RECIPES FOR LIFE®

FROM THE KITCHENS OF

HEALTHY CHOICE®

FOODS

CY DeCOSSE
INCORPORATED

A COWLES MAGAZINES COMPANY

TABLE OF CONTENTS

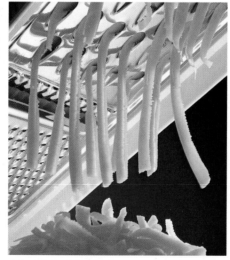

NUTRITION FOR LIFE

NUTRITION FOR LIFE

Healthy cooking and making good food choices are simple—once you know the basics of good nutrition.

Dietary Guidelines

The Dietary Guidelines for Americans are seven basic principles for developing and maintaining a healthier diet and reducing your risk of diet-related diseases. The Guidelines, established by the U.S. Department of Agriculture (USDA) and the U.S. Department of Health and Human Services (HHS), emphasize balance, variety and moderation in the total diet. The Dietary Guidelines for Americans are:

◆ Eat a variety of foods.

◆ Maintain healthy weight.

◆ Choose a diet low in fat, saturated fat and cholesterol.

◆ Choose a diet with plenty of vegetables, fruits and grain products.

◆ Use sugars only in moderation.

◆ Use salt and sodium only in moderation.

◆ If you drink alcoholic beverages, do so in moderation.

The Food Guide Pyramid

To help put the Dietary Guidelines into action, the USDA developed the Food Guide Pyramid. The pyramid is not a rigid prescription, but a guide that lets you choose a healthy diet that is right for you. Foods grouped together provide similar nutrients and calories, and no single food group is more important than another.

The pyramid emphasizes the importance of eating a variety of foods in moderate amounts from each food group. By focusing on the total diet, it shows that there are no good foods or bad foods. In other words, it's o.k. to have bacon and eggs for breakfast occasionally. Just don't have them every day, and balance out that high-fat, high-cholesterol meal with more healthful food choices over the course of the day.

New Labeling Requirements

The Food and Drug Administration (FDA) has put into place new food product labeling regulations which are designed to help you make better decisions when purchasing foods and planning your meals.

Recipes for Life from the kitchens of Healthy Choice® shows you how to use both the pyramid and the new packaging information to provide yourself with a healthy diet. ▲

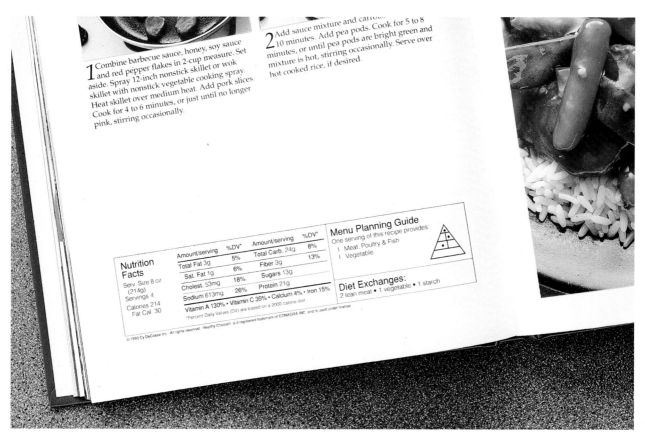

Nutritional Information

Each recipe in this book is followed by a Nutrition Facts chart and diet exchanges. The Nutrition Facts chart is similar to those that will appear on food product labels. The diet exchange system is used by people with diabetes and persons on a weight-control diet, to estimate the calories, protein, carbohydrate and fat content of a food or meal. Diet exchanges are based on exchange lists and are not the same as pyramid servings.

If alternate ingredients are given in the recipe's ingredient list, such as a choice between cholesterol-free egg product and egg, the nutritional analysis applies to the first ingredient listed. Optional ingredients are not included in the analysis. For pasta and rice, the nutritional information applies to the plain, boiled item without salt or fat added.

Recipe serving sizes are based on federal reference numbers for serving sizes.

Metric Conversion

For guidelines and hints for converting these recipes into metrics, refer to the charts on pages 252 and 253.

The Pyramid in This Book

Each recipe in this book includes a Menu Planning Guide that shows the number of servings from each pyramid group that one serving of that recipe provides. A daily total of these "pyramid servings" shows how your diet compares to the USDA recommendations.

When the tip of the pyramid has a dot, the item may contain added fat or fat beyond the natural fat content of lean or low-fat items in the food groups. Refer to the Nutrition Facts chart to check the total amount of fat per serving. A tip with a dot may also indicate that the recipe contains added sugar. Refer to the recipe to determine the number of teaspoons of sugar you will eat.

With each menu in the Healthy Menus section of this book, you will find a small diagram of the food pyramid. The numbers within the pyramid tell you the number of servings that meal satisfies for each food group.

The number of servings is rounded to the nearest half. If no figures appear next to or within the pyramid, it means that serving sizes are negligible.

If the tip of the pyramid has no dot, a serving contains less than 3 grams added fat or less than 1 teaspoon added sugar. ▲

7

THE FOOD GUIDE PYRAMID

Nutrition for Life

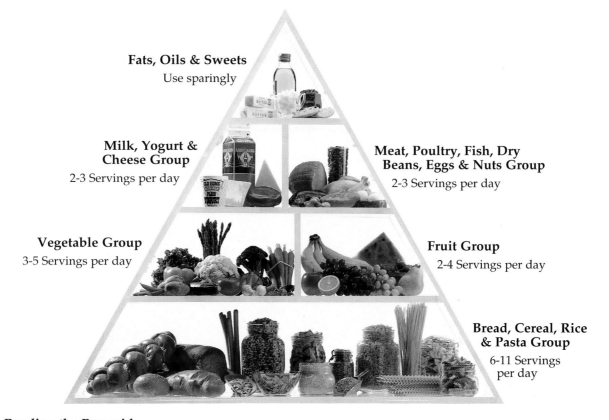

Fats, Oils & Sweets
Use sparingly

**Milk, Yogurt &
Cheese Group**
2-3 Servings per day

**Meat, Poultry, Fish, Dry
Beans, Eggs & Nuts Group**
2-3 Servings per day

Vegetable Group
3-5 Servings per day

Fruit Group
2-4 Servings per day

**Bread, Cereal, Rice
& Pasta Group**
6-11 Servings
per day

Reading the Pyramid

It's easy to follow the Food Guide Pyramid.

The bottom of the pyramid shows complex carbohydrates—the bread, cereal, rice and pasta group—at 6-11 servings a day. This group should be the foundation of a healthy diet.

The second level is made up of fruits and vegetables. We need to eat 3-5 servings of vegetables and 2-4 servings of fruit each day.

The third level is divided equally between milk, yogurt and cheese (2-3 servings a day) and meat, poultry, fish, beans, eggs and nuts (2-3 servings a day).

Most supermarkets now carry skim or low-fat milk and buttermilk; low-fat or nonfat yogurt, cottage cheese or ricotta cheese; and other low-fat cheeses.

A large variety of lean cuts of meat is also available in most stores. The leanest cuts of beef are the round, loin, sirloin and chuck arm. Pork tenderloin, center loin or lean ham, and all cuts of veal, except ground veal, are relatively lean. For lamb, the leanest cuts are the leg, loin and foreshanks. Chicken and turkey with the skin removed and most fish are lean meat choices.

The tip of the pyramid shows fats, oils and sweets. These include foods such as salad dressings, cream, butter, margarine, sugars, soft drinks and candies. Use them sparingly.

Build a diet of good food choices based on complex carbohydrates, and limit your intake of high-fat foods. The recipes in this book make it easy to fit nutritious meals into a busy schedule. And you don't have to choose between good taste and good nutrition. You can have them both.

Balancing Your Diet

The number of servings per day that is right for you depends on the amount of calories you need to maintain your best weight. The USDA recommends the following calorie levels per day: 1600 calories for many sedentary women and some older adults; 2200 calories for most children, teenage girls, active women and many sedentary men; and 2800 calories for teenage boys, many active men and some very active women. Each person's body is different, however, and you may need more or less depending on your age, sex, size, activity level and medical condition.

For example, if your calorie intake level is in the lower range, choose the smaller number of servings in each food group. Or, if you are very active, choose the larger number of servings in each group. (See chart on page 25.) ▲

What counts as a serving?

You may be surprised. Use this chart to determine how your food intake compares to servings on the pyramid.

For combination foods, use your best judgment in estimating which food groups they fall into. For example, a large serving of pasta with tomato sauce and cheese could count in the bread group, the vegetable group and the milk group.

Milk, Yogurt & Cheese Group

1 cup low-fat milk or yogurt

2 ounces processed cheese, preferably reduced fat

1½ ounces natural cheese, preferably reduced fat

Meat, Poultry & Fish Group

2-3 ounces cooked lean meat, poultry or fish

½ cup cooked dry beans, 1 egg or 2 tablespoons peanut butter count as 1 ounce lean meat

Vegetable Group

1 cup raw leafy vegetables

¾ cup vegetable juice

½ cup other vegetables, cooked or raw

Fruit Group

¾ cup fruit juice

½ cup chopped, cooked or canned fruit

1 medium apple, banana or orange

Bread, Cereal, Rice & Pasta Group

1 muffin, dinner roll or slice bread

1 ounce ready-to-eat cereal

½ cup cooked cereal, rice or pasta

HOW TO READ A LABEL

Food labels are more than just names on a package. They contain a wealth of information, and if you understand labels, you can make better food choices.

Three important features of food labels are: Descriptors, Health Claims and "Nutrition Facts."

- **Descriptors,** or nutrient-content claims, are terms like "cholesterol-free" and "light."

- **Health Claims** are statements allowed on some products that meet certain requirements. Research has shown that some foods or nutrients may help reduce the risk of certain diseases or health-related conditions. There are seven different health claims allowed on food labels.

- **"Nutrition Facts"** is the part of the label that provides per serving nutritional information for the product (i.e., serving sizes, calories and daily values for nutrients).

Descriptors

Terms like "low-fat" and "low-sodium" have been appearing on food labels for years, but these terms have not had standard definitions until recently. Now that new food labeling laws have been established by the Food and Drug Administration (FDA), specific definitions for all descriptors are spelled out. Some of the more common descriptors are:

Free (e.g., "cholesterol-free")—A product termed "free" must contain no amount or only a very small amount of that substance. For example:

- "Calorie-free" means less than 5 calories per serving.

- "Sugar-free" means less than ½ gram sugar per serving.

Low (e.g., "low in fat")— The term "low" can be used with fat, saturated fat, cholesterol, sodium and calories. For example:

- "Low-fat" has 3 or less grams fat per serving.

- "Low-sodium" has 140 or less milligrams sodium per serving.

Lean and extra lean— These terms describe the fat content of meat, poultry and seafood.

- "Lean" means less than 10 grams fat, less than 4 grams saturated fat and less than 95 milligrams cholesterol per serving.

- "Extra lean" means less than 5 grams fat, less than 2 grams saturated fat and less than 95 milligrams cholesterol per serving.

High (e.g., "high in vitamin C")—This term means the product contains 20% or more of the Daily Value for that nutrient per serving.

Good Source (e.g., "good source of calcium")—The use of this term indicates one serving contains 10-19% of the Daily Value for a nutrient.

Reduced or less (e.g., "reduced in saturated fat" or "25% less fat")— This term can appear on a product that contains less than 25% of a nutrient or calories when compared to a similar product.

Light—This term has two definitions:

- a product contains one-third fewer calories or half the fat.

- the sodium content of a low-calorie, low-fat food has been reduced by 50%.

"Light" can also describe properties like texture and color, providing the intent is explained (e.g., "light brown sugar" and "light and fluffy").

For more information, write to: Food Labeling Education Information Center, National Agricultural Library, Room 304, 10301 Baltimore Blvd., Beltsville, MD 20705-2351

Health Claims

If food products meet specific criteria for fat, saturated fat, cholesterol and sodium, manufacturers may be able to feature health claims on labels in seven areas.

- ◆ Fat and cancer—A low-fat diet has been linked to helping reduce the risk of some types of cancer.

- ◆ Calcium and osteoporosis—A diet adequate in calcum may help reduce the risk of osteoporosis.

- ◆ Saturated fat and cholesterol and heart disease— Foods low in saturated fat and cholesterol may reduce the risk of heart disease.

- ◆ Fiber and cancer—Diets low in fat and high in fiber may reduce the risk of some types of cancer.

- ◆ Fiber and heart disease—Along with eating a diet that is low in saturated fat and cholesterol, fiber (particularly soluble fiber) may help reduce the risk of heart disease.

- ◆ Sodium and high blood pressure—A low-sodium, low-salt diet may help prevent high blood pressure.

- ◆ Fruits and vegetables and cancer—A diet high in fruits and vegetables and low in fat may help lower the risk of some types of cancer.

A sample health claim might read: "While many factors affect heart disease, diets low in saturated fat and cholesterol may reduce the risk of this disease."

Nutrition Facts

Nutritional information on food products will appear in a version of the following format:

- ◆ **Nutrition Facts** state serving size, servings per container and amount per serving of calories, calories from fat and other nutrients.

A food can be called a "good source" of a vitamin or mineral if it contains more than 10% of the Daily Value for that nutrient. For example, this product is a good source of calcium.

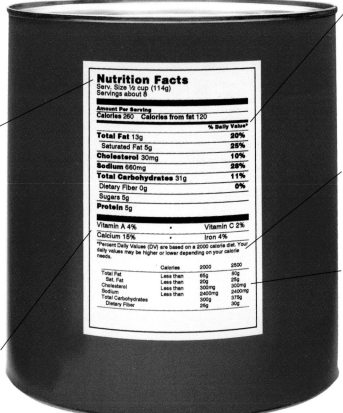

Nutrition Facts
Serv. Size ½ cup (114g)
Servings about 8

Amount Per Serving

Calories 260   Calories from fat 120

	% Daily Value*
Total Fat 13g	**20%**
Saturated Fat 5g	**25%**
Cholesterol 30mg	**10%**
Sodium 660mg	**28%**
Total Carbohydrates 31g	**11%**
Dietary Fiber 0g	**0%**
Sugars 5g	
Protein 5g	

Vitamin A 4%	•	Vitamin C 2%
Calcium 15%	•	Iron 4%

*Percent Daily Values (DV) are based on a 2000 calorie diet. Your daily values may be higher or lower depending on your calorie needs.

		Calories	2000	2500
Total Fat	Less than		65g	80g
Sat. Fat	Less than		20g	25g
Cholesterol	Less than		300mg	300mg
Sodium	Less than		2400mg	2400mg
Total Carbohydrates			300g	375g
Dietary Fiber			25g	30g

- ◆ **% Daily Value**
  This new term gives you an idea of what percentage of the day's worth of these nutrients comes from this food. The percentages of the Daily Value of fat, saturated fat, cholesterol, sodium, total carbohydrates and dietary fiber are based on a 2,000-calorie-per-day diet.

The footnote tells you that "your Daily Value may vary depending on your calorie needs." For instance, one serving of this product accounts for 20% of the recommended amount of fat.

The Dietary Guidelines recommend that no more than 30% of your calories come from fat. So, if you are eating 2,000 calories a day, your total fat intake should be less than 65 grams. One serving of this product has 13 grams of fat.

NUTRIENT LISTINGS

The following nutrients are usually found on food labels.

Fats

You need a certain amount of fat in your diet for good health. Fats give food flavor, and they also provide energy and help the body absorb and use fat-soluble vitamins. Too much fat in the diet, however, can increase the fat levels in the bloodstream of some people. It also contributes to obesity.

There are three types of fats: saturated, polyunsaturated and monounsaturated. These fats differ in the amount of hydrogen they contain. Saturated fats contain the most hydrogen and polyunsaturated the least. Saturated fats tend to raise the blood cholesterol level in certain people.

Foods that contain fat have a mix of all three types of fats. Saturated fats are found in animal foods and oils, such as palm kernel and coconut.

Polyunsaturated fats are usually liquid at room temperature, like corn and soybean oils. Soft margarines contain polyunsaturated fats, too. These fats may actually break down saturated fats and reduce blood cholesterol.

Monounsaturated fats are found in olive oil, canola oil, peanut oil, vegetable shortening and stick margarine. They may be even more effective than polyunsaturated fats in reducing blood cholesterol. Experts recommend substituting monounsaturated fats for saturated fats in the diet as much as possible.

Cholesterol

Cholesterol is a fatlike substance that is found in foods from animal sources, such as meat, poultry, fish, egg yolks, milk and milk products. Cholesterol is not found in fruits, vegetables, breads and cereals, nuts, seeds, or dry beans and peas.

Your body needs some cholesterol for good health, but it makes enough on its own. The foods you eat can also affect how much cholesterol is in your blood. Eating too much saturated fat and cholesterol raises blood cholesterol levels in certain people. High blood cholesterol levels can increase the risk of heart disease.

Sodium

Sodium is important for maintaining body fluids and proper nerve function. However, many of us consume more sodium than we need. Eating less sodium may be better for your heart and your blood pressure. The National Research Council recommends daily intake be limited to 2400 miligrams.

Most of the sodium in your diet comes from salt already in the prepared foods you buy and the salt that you add to food in cooking and at the table. Just one teaspoon of table salt contains 2132 milligrams of sodium.

The recipes in this book use salt and products containing sodium, such as broths, but they also show you how to season with herbs, spices and other flavorings to enhance the natural flavors of food. If you are on a sodium-restricted diet, simply replace full-salt products with many of their reduced-salt counterparts.

Calories

A calorie is a measure of the energy supplied by the foods you eat and drink. Calories come from carbohydrates, protein, fats and alcohol. If you eat the right amount of calories and exercise regularly, you should burn off all the calories you eat and maintain a healthy weight.

Some foods are higher in calories than other foods. For example, foods that have more fat and sugar may have more calories. The way a food is prepared can also make a big difference in the number of calories it contains. Use low-fat cooking techniques when you cook (see pages 16 to 19).

Protein

Protein is needed to build and repair body tissues. All proteins are made up of amino acids. The body needs 22 different amino acids to function properly. Nine of these are called "essential amino acids" because the body cannot make them. We must get them from the foods we eat.

A food that supplies all the amino acids in the right amounts is a "complete protein." Foods from animals —milk, cheese, eggs and meat—are complete proteins. Plant foods are "incomplete proteins," so they must be combined with other foods in order to get the right amount of amino acids. A vegetarian would need to plan carefully to meet protein needs.

Carbohydrates & Fiber

Carbohydrates provide energy. They come in two forms: simple and complex. Simple carbohydrates (sugars) are found in fruits, juices and refined sugars. Complex carbohydrates (starches and fiber) are found in breads, cereals, potatoes, pasta and beans.

Fiber keeps your digestive tract healthy. Foods that contain fiber are usually low in calories, since fiber is found only in foods that come from plants. Fruits, vegetables, whole-grain cereals, dry peas, nuts and seeds are good sources of fiber.

NUTRIENT LISTINGS

Calcium

Calcium is a bone builder and aids in the prevention of osteoporosis. Yet Americans consume far less than the 800 milligrams per day recommended for most adults over age 25. Calcium is present in low-fat dairy products; leafy green vegetables and broccoli; some fish, like canned salmon; and oysters.

Potassium

Potassium is important for maintaining strong bones and teeth. It works with sodium to balance body fluids and keep nerves and muscles running smoothly. Good sources of potassium are fruits and vegetables, meats, milk, whole grains and legumes. Especially good sources are bananas, orange juice, milk and potatoes.

Iron

Iron's primary purpose is to build red blood cells. It also carries oxygen to the brain. Iron is found in many foods. Meat, fish and poultry are good sources, as are fortified cereals. Vitamin C increases iron absorption.

Vitamin A

Vitamin A is essential for healthy eyes, skin and other tissues. Beta carotene in foods like carrots and dark green leafy vegetables is converted to vitamin A and could have a role in cancer prevention. Good sources of vitamin A are milk, sweet potatoes, carrots, broccoli and fruits such as cantaloupe and apricots.

Vitamin C

Vitamin C puts strength in your bones and teeth, and promotes healthy gum tissue. It is also responsible for fighting infection. Fruits and vegetables are primary sources of vitamin C, especially citrus fruit and juice, bell peppers, green leafy vegetables, broccoli, strawberries and tomatoes.

Thiamin

Thiamin, or vitamin B-1, helps the body cells convert starches and sugars to energy. Thiamin also nourishes the nervous system and muscles, and regulates appetite and attitude. Top food sources are lean pork, wheat bran, nuts, whole wheat flour, cornmeal and enriched rice.

Riboflavin

Riboflavin, another B complex vitamin, helps body cells use oxygen to get energy from amino acids, fats and carbohydrates. It is found in almonds, lean meat, breads, mushrooms, turnip greens and wheat bran.

Niacin

Niacin, also a B complex vitamin, works to produce energy within the cells in exactly the amount the body needs at any particular time. Good sources of niacin are lean meats, poultry, fish, mushrooms, nuts and dairy products.

MENU TIPS: REDUCING FATS

Here are some basic food preparation tips to help you reduce the amount of fats in your diet. Remember, though, that it is your total diet, not the fat content of individual foods, that is most important.

Salad Dressings

Choose oil-free salad dressings or make your own with low-fat or non-fat buttermilk or yogurt. Reduce the amount of oil in homemade salad dressings by replacing half with tomato juice, flavored vinegar or water.

Meats, Poultry & Fish

Use lean cuts of meat and extra-lean ground beef. Choose low-fat processed meats. Remove skin from all poultry before serving, since two-thirds of poultry's fat is hidden in the skin. Marinate meats, poultry and fish before cooking; marinades help hold in easily lost moisture when cooking leaner cuts and eliminate the need for a sauce.

Sauces

Rather than use oil or butter to make sauces, thicken liquids with cornstarch or flour. Whisk the thickener into a small amount of cold water—use 1 tablespoon cornstarch or 2 tablespoons flour per 1 cup liquid—then add to sauce and simmer until thickened. If you like, try puréeing cooked vegetables in a blender; then season lightly.

16

Breads

When shopping for breads and rolls, choose bagels made without egg yolks, English muffins and whole-grain breads more often. Eat high-fat croissants, muffins, sweet rolls, coffee cakes and doughnuts less frequently.

Dairy Products

Choose low-fat dairy products, such as nonfat or low-fat buttermilk and yogurt, skim milk and low-fat cheeses. When used in baking or cooking, they generally taste and act similarly to their high-fat cousins.

Grains, Vegetables & Pasta

Move grains, vegetables and pasta to the center of the plate; use meat as a side dish in small quantities instead of as the focal point.

Eggs

Reduce your consumption of egg yolks. Try using cholesterol-free egg product for baking, or substitute 2 egg whites for each whole egg in most baked goods.

Stocks

Make your own chicken and meat stocks by simmering poultry or meat bones in water. Refrigerate overnight to allow any fat to solidify on the top; then skim it off. Remove and discard skin from poultry.

TECHNIQUES FOR COOKING WITH LESS FAT

After you have made good food choices, you need to prepare those foods in a healthy manner. Avoid high-fat cooking techniques like frying and deep-fat frying. The following techniques will ensure that your meals are as nutritious as possible:

Braising is a method of cooking in which food is quickly browned and then simmered in liquid. It allows deep flavors to emerge and is especially effective to tenderize leaner cuts of meat.

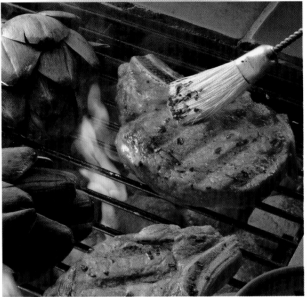

Broiling means speedy cooking directly under the heat source. It is ideal for thin pieces of meat, vegetables, or other foods that can dry out quickly. Marinating foods prior to broiling helps keep them moist.

Grilling, an outdoor summer favorite, is now possible year-round with indoor stovetop grills. To ensure flavor and moistness, marinate foods for 30 minutes beforehand, then brush frequently with reserved marinade while grilling.

Poaching, cooking food in a simmering liquid, keeps it moist and tender without adding fat. Favorite poaching liquids are wines, sherry, fruit juices, broths and water. For an elegant low-fat sauce, poaching liquid can be reduced, thickened with cornstarch and spooned over the poached food.

Roasting winter vegetables and leaner cuts of meat in a moderate oven (300 to 350°F) tenderizes them. Since roasting is a dry cooking technique, stocks or broths are often poured in the bottom of the roaster and the roaster is tented with foil to keep in moisture.

Microwaving is moist-heat cooking. Foods can be prepared with no fat. In addition, microwaving is a great way to preserve vitamins and color in vegetables.

Steaming preserves many more nutrients than boiling and requires no added fat, making it one of the healthiest cooking techniques. It is especially good for whole fish, chopped vegetables and large vegetables like artichokes or asparagus.

Sautéing and Stir-frying are cooking methods that use small amounts of fat or cooking oil in a skillet or wok. The food is constantly stirred as it cooks over medium-high to high heat. This quick cooking seals in moisture and allows food to retain much of its flavor, color and texture.

Exercise

Regular exercise is an essential part of a healthy life-style. Exercise helps reduce stress and keeps weight under control.

Make exercise a regular part of your commitment to a healthier life-style. Warm up slowly, pace yourself during exercise and stretch carefully after cooling down. Look closely at your current fitness level, and be patient with your progress. Remember to check with your doctor before beginning any exercise program.

Travel Tips

When traveling, book a hotel room with a kitchenette or refrigerator to save on restaurant meals. Stock it with low-fat breakfast foods, lunches and snacks.

Check to see whether your airline offers a special diet menu. Most major airlines carry an assortment of dishes that include low-calorie, low-fat and low-cholesterol, and low-sodium items. Take along bags of healthy snacks like rice cakes, fresh vegetable sticks or fruit.

Eating Out

Call ahead to see what nutritious choices the restaurant offers. Teach yourself to recognize low-fat menu items, such as lean cuts of meat, poultry and fish that are baked or broiled without sauces or added fats; side dishes of steamed or stir-fried vegetables; and fruit desserts without high-fat crusts or toppings.

Order a salad with low-fat dressing, or a lemon wedge and balsamic vinegar. Top a plain baked potato with low-calorie salad dressing and a salt-free seasoning.

Before going to a party, eat a little at home. If you arrive hungry, you'll probably eat more. If you eat a small low-calorie meal at home first, you'll be less tempted.

Weight Control

Making good food choices can bring weight loss, but the real purpose of healthy eating is to promote health and well-being. If you want a weight-loss diet tailored to your needs, consult your doctor or dietitian to make sure the recipes in this book fit your personal needs.

Fight cravings. There's a difference between a genuine hunger for food and a psychological craving for food. Have an assortment of low-fat, yet satisfying, snacks on hand.

Never skip a meal. Breakfast is important for starting the day with sufficient fuel. If you skip breakfast, you might end up snacking on high-fat doughnuts at 10 a.m.

Shopping

Healthier eating doesn't mean buying more expensive foods or spending more time in the kitchen. A variety of convenience products like canned cooked beans and low-fat pasta sauces are available on most supermarket shelves. With the growing public awareness of nutrition, manufacturers are providing shoppers with a larger selection of sensible choices that fit busy life-styles.

To avoid impulse buys at the store, plan a healthy menu and shop for just the items on your grocery list. Include plenty of fresh fruits and vegetables, and remember to read labels carefully, too (see pages 10 and 11 for more tips).

HEALTHY MENUS

HEALTHY MENUS

Keep the food pyramid in mind when you plan your menus. Once you've decided how many servings from each food group are right for you, try to get something from each group in your meals. Choose snacks that will contribute to rounding out the number of servings you require. For example, if you have a bowl of cereal with milk and a glass of orange juice for breakfast, you can figure that you've gotten one serving from each of the bread, milk and fruit groups. You might snack on some carrots later in the day to get a vegetable serving.

Think in terms of a whole day's worth of eating. Not everyone can plan to eat a completely balanced meal every time they sit down. You may only have time for a bagel and apple at lunch. The balance needs to come over the course of the day or several days. Satisfy as many servings from the pyramid as you can throughout the day.

The menus provided for you in this book show you healthy, hearty ways to plan a meal. They are simple guidelines to help you get started in planning healthy menus on your own using these and your own favorite recipes.

Menu 1

▲ *Brandy Pepper Steaks*
Boiled New Potatoes (5 oz.)
Steamed Broccoli Spears (3 spears)
Devil's Food Cupcake
(from mix)

Number of Daily Servings Provided

Menu 2

▲ *Orange Chicken Véronique*
Spinach Salad
1 cup raw spinach, ¼ cup sliced fresh mushrooms,
¼ thinly sliced red onion, 1 tbsp. light French dressing

White Rice (½ cup)
▲ *Blackberry Pavlovas*

Number of Daily Servings Provided

▲ Denotes Recipe in Card Series

These Healthy Menus are based on the following standards:

◆ 2000 calories per day

◆ No more than 30 percent total calories from fat (65 g per day)

◆ Less than 300 mg cholesterol per day

◆ 2400 mg or less sodium per day

Each menu will feature a recipe or recipes from the book. The menu will be completed with items that are easy to prepare and complement the recipes. (Analysis of nonbook items comes from USDA Handbook No. 8 "Composition of Foods.")

The food pyramid will appear next to each menu. You can see at a glance how many servings it provides from each food group in the pyramid.

How Many Servings Are Right for Me?

The Food Guide Pyramid shows a range of servings for each major food group. (See pages 7 and 8 for servings information.) The number of servings that is right for you depends on how many calories you need. Almost everyone should eat at least the lowest number of servings in the ranges.

The chart to the right shows examples for three different calorie intakes. Recommended amounts of total fat for the day are stated in grams. Some of the fat you eat each day, as in 2% milk, a muffin or an egg, will occur in foods from the five major food groups. Other fats, such as margarine or salad dressing, do not fall within the five food groups. You must consider both sources of fat in your daily intake.

The teaspoons of sugar listed in the chart provide a guideline for how much added sugar is appropriate within your total diet. Added sugar includes foods such as table sugar, honey, jelly or syrup.

Sample Diets for a Day			
	Approx. 1600 calories	Approx. 2200 calories	Approx. 2800 calories
Bread Group Servings	6	9	11
Vegetable Group Servings	3	4	5
Fruit Group Servings	2	3	4
Milk Group Servings[1]	2-3	2-3	2-3
Meat Group Servings	2-3	2-3	3-4
Total Fat (g)[2]	53	73	93
Total Added Sugar (tsp.)[3]	6	12	18

[1]Women who are breastfeeding, teenagers and young adults to age 24 need 3 servings.
[2]One serving equals 5 grams.
[3]One serving equals 1 teaspoon.

Menu 1

▲ **Brandy Pepper Steaks**
Boiled New Potatoes (5 oz.)
Steamed Broccoli Spears (3 spears)
Devil's Food Cupcake
(from mix)

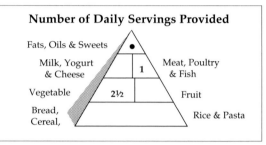

Number of Daily Servings Provided

Fats, Oils & Sweets	●	
Milk, Yogurt & Cheese	1	Meat, Poultry & Fish
Vegetable	2½	Fruit
Bread, Cereal,		Rice & Pasta

Menu 2

▲ **Orange Chicken Véronique**

Spinach Salad
1 cup spinach, ¼ cup sliced mushrooms,
¼ cup red onion strips, 1 tbsp. light French dressing

White Rice (½ cup)

▲ **Blackberry Pavlovas**

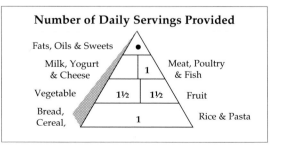

Number of Daily Servings Provided

Fats, Oils & Sweets	●	
Milk, Yogurt & Cheese	1	Meat, Poultry & Fish
Vegetable	1½	1½ Fruit
Bread, Cereal,	1	Rice & Pasta

▲ Denotes Recipe in Book

Menu 3

▲ **Chinese-style Steamed Trout**

Brown Rice (½ cup)

Onion & Orange Salad
*¼ cup red onion rings, ½ cup orange segments,
1 tbsp. vinaigrette, 1 leaf lettuce*

Lemon Sherbet (½ cup)

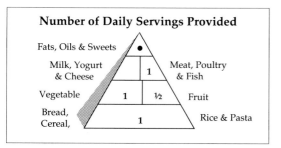

Number of Daily Servings Provided

Fats, Oils & Sweets	●	
Milk, Yogurt & Cheese	1	Meat, Poultry & Fish
Vegetable	1	½ Fruit
Bread, Cereal,	1	Rice & Pasta

Menu 4

▲ **Tomato Cheese Pie**

Melon Ball Salad (1 cup)
honeydew, cantaloupe, watermelon

Angel Food Cake (1 slice)
(from mix)
with Chocolate Syrup (1 tbsp.)

Number of Daily Servings Provided

Fats, Oils & Sweets	●	
Milk, Yogurt & Cheese	½	Meat, Poultry & Fish
Vegetable		2 Fruit
Bread, Cereal,	1	Rice & Pasta

▲ **Denotes Recipe in Book**

Menu 5

▲ *Herbed Flank Steak Sandwiches*

▲ *Rosemary New Potatoes & Beans*

Fresh Fruit Plate (1½ cups)
orange segments, grapes, sliced strawberries

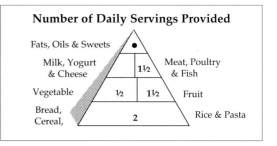

Number of Daily Servings Provided

Fats, Oils & Sweets ●

Milk, Yogurt & Cheese — 1½ — Meat, Poultry & Fish

Vegetable — ½ — 1½ — Fruit

Bread, Cereal, — 2 — Rice & Pasta

Menu 6

▲ *Szechuan Barbecue Pork*
& Vegetables

Chinese Noodles (¾ cup)

Fortune Cookie

Mandarin Orange Segments (½ cup)

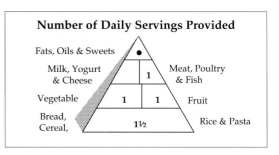

Number of Daily Servings Provided

Fats, Oils & Sweets ●

Milk, Yogurt & Cheese — 1 — Meat, Poultry & Fish

Vegetable — 1 — 1 — Fruit

Bread, Cereal, — 1½ — Rice & Pasta

▲ **Denotes Recipe in Book**

Menu 7

▲ *Turkey Marsala*

▲ *Brown Rice with Toasted Pine Nuts*

Fresh Tomato (2 slices)

Low-fat Vanilla Ice Cream ◆ *(½ cup) with Fresh Raspberries (⅓ cup)*

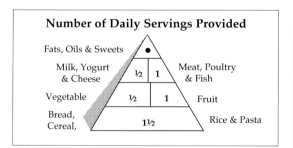

Number of Daily Servings Provided

Fats, Oils & Sweets	●		
Milk, Yogurt & Cheese	½	1	Meat, Poultry & Fish
Vegetable	½	1	Fruit
Bread, Cereal,		1½	Rice & Pasta

Menu 8

▲ *Vegetable-Shrimp Stir-fry*

White Rice (½ cup)

▲ *Apple & Apricot Poached Pears*

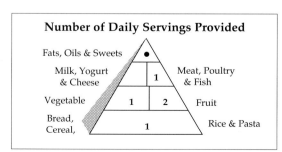

Number of Daily Servings Provided

Fats, Oils & Sweets	●		
Milk, Yogurt & Cheese		1	Meat, Poultry & Fish
Vegetable	1	2	Fruit
Bread, Cereal,		1	Rice & Pasta

▲ **Denotes Recipe in Book**

◆ Look for Healthy Choice® products at your favorite supermarket.

Menu 9

▲ *Apple-Sage Stuffed Pork Loin Roast*

Steamed Asparagus Spears (5 oz.)

Wild Rice (½ cup)

Baked Apple

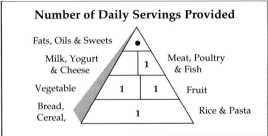

Number of Daily Servings Provided

Fats, Oils & Sweets ●		
Milk, Yogurt & Cheese	1	Meat, Poultry & Fish
Vegetable	1 | 1	Fruit
Bread, Cereal,	1	Rice & Pasta

Menu 10

▲ *Chicken Gumbo*

White Rice (½ cup)

Pineapple Nonfat Frozen Yogurt (½ cup)

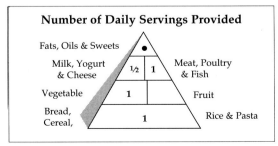

Number of Daily Servings Provided

Fats, Oils & Sweets ●		
Milk, Yogurt & Cheese	½ | 1	Meat, Poultry & Fish
Vegetable	1	Fruit
Bread, Cereal,	1	Rice & Pasta

▲ **Denotes Recipe in Book**

Menu 11

▲ **Orange-sauced Roughy**

Rice Pilaf (½ cup)

Steamed Snow Pea Pods (½ cup)

▲ **Pineapple Carrot Cake**

Number of Daily Servings Provided

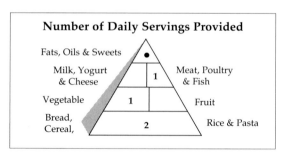

Fats, Oils & Sweets ●

Milk, Yogurt & Cheese — 1 — Meat, Poultry & Fish

Vegetable — 1 — Fruit

Bread, Cereal, — 2 — Rice & Pasta

Menu 12

▲ **Three-cheese Stuffed Manicotti**

2 Bread Sticks

Lettuce Salad
½ cup lettuce, ¼ cup cherry tomatoes,
2 tbsp. sliced mushrooms, 2 tbsp. shaved carrots,
1 tbsp. low-fat vinaigrette

Low-fat Neapolitan Ice Cream ◆ (½ cup)

Number of Daily Servings Provided

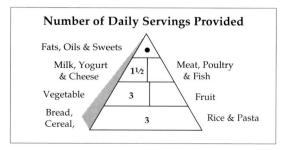

Fats, Oils & Sweets ●

Milk, Yogurt & Cheese — 1½ — Meat, Poultry & Fish

Vegetable — 3 — Fruit

Bread, Cereal, — 3 — Rice & Pasta

▲ **Denotes Recipe in Book**

◆ Look for Healthy Choice® products at your favorite supermarket.

Menu 13

▲ **Southwestern-style Pot Roast**

**Baked Potato (5 oz.)
with Plain Yogurt (1 tbsp.)**

Melon Slices
watermelon, honeydew, cantaloupe

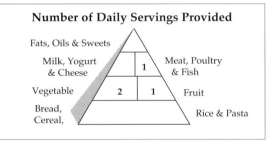

Number of Daily Servings Provided

Fats, Oils & Sweets		
Milk, Yogurt & Cheese	1	Meat, Poultry & Fish
Vegetable	2	1	Fruit
Bread, Cereal,		Rice & Pasta

Menu 14

▲ **Veal Scallops with Mandarin Orange Sauce**

Steamed Green Beans (½ cup)

▲ **Whole Wheat Onion Bread**

Raspberry Sorbet (½ cup)

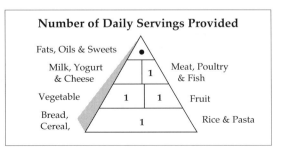

Number of Daily Servings Provided

Fats, Oils & Sweets ●		
Milk, Yogurt & Cheese	1	Meat, Poultry & Fish
Vegetable	1	1	Fruit
Bread, Cereal,	1	Rice & Pasta

▲ **Denotes Recipe in Book**

Menu 15

▲ *Lime & Cumin*
Cornish Game Hens

Steamed Baby Carrots (½ cup)

Boiled New Potatoes (5 oz.)

▲ *Tropical Fruit Combo*

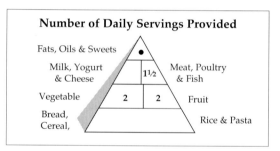

Number of Daily Servings Provided

- Fats, Oils & Sweets ●
- Milk, Yogurt & Cheese — 1½
- Meat, Poultry & Fish
- Vegetable — 2
- Fruit — 2
- Bread, Cereal,
- Rice & Pasta

Menu 16

▲ *Saffron Shrimp & Tomato*

Spinach Salad
1 cup spinach, ¼ cup red onion rings,
1 tbsp. low-fat vinaigrette

Chocolate Cake (1 piece)
(from mix)

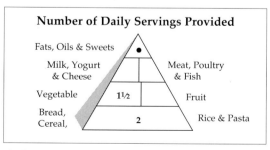

Number of Daily Servings Provided

- Fats, Oils & Sweets ●
- Milk, Yogurt & Cheese
- Meat, Poultry & Fish
- Vegetable — 1½
- Fruit
- Bread, Cereal,
- Rice & Pasta — 2

▲ **Denotes Recipe in Book**

Menu 17

▲ **Ragout of Lamb**

Couscous (½ cup)

Romaine Salad
1 cup romaine, ¼ cup red onion rings,
¼ cup cherry tomatoes, 2 tbsp. sliced mushrooms,
1 tbsp. fat-free Italian dressing

**Lemon Sherbet (½ cup)
with Thin Wafer Cookie**

Number of Daily Servings Provided

Fats, Oils & Sweets	●	
Milk, Yogurt & Cheese	1	Meat, Poultry & Fish
Vegetable	3	Fruit
Bread, Cereal,	1	Rice & Pasta

Menu 18

▲ **Spring Lemon Chicken**

Steamed Asparagus Spears (5 oz.)

**Boiled New Potatoes (5 oz.)
with Chives**

▲ **Apple Raisin Bran Muffins**

Sliced Fresh Peach

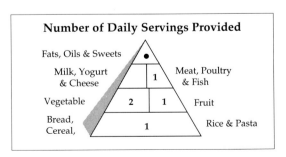

Number of Daily Servings Provided

Fats, Oils & Sweets	●	
Milk, Yogurt & Cheese	1	Meat, Poultry & Fish
Vegetable	2 1	Fruit
Bread, Cereal,	1	Rice & Pasta

▲ **Denotes Recipe in Book**

Menu 19

▲ *Fillet of Sole Almondine*

Baked Potato (5 oz.)
with Plain Yogurt (1 tbsp.)

Mixed Vegetables (½ cup)

Low-Fat Vanilla
Ice Cream ◆ *(½ cup)*
with Sliced Strawberries (⅓ cup)

Number of Daily Servings Provided

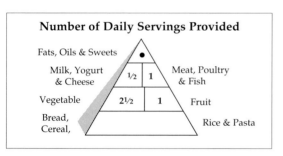

Fats, Oils & Sweets	●	
Milk, Yogurt & Cheese	½	1	Meat, Poultry & Fish
Vegetable	2½	1	Fruit
Bread, Cereal,		Rice & Pasta

Menu 20

Grilled Jumbo Shrimp (4 oz.)

▲ *Polynesian Pilaf*

Sourdough Bread (2 slices)

▲ *Fudgy Cheesecake*
with Cherry Sauce

Number of Daily Servings Provided

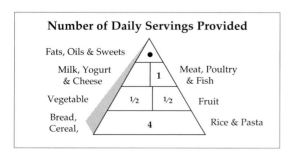

Fats, Oils & Sweets	●	
Milk, Yogurt & Cheese		1	Meat, Poultry & Fish
Vegetable	½	½	Fruit
Bread, Cereal,	4		Rice & Pasta

▲ **Denotes Recipe in Book**

◆ Look for Healthy Choice® products at your favorite supermarket.

Menu 21

▲ **Barbecued Chicken Sandwich**

Broccoli & Cauliflower Salad (½ cup) with Yogurt-Dill Dressing (1 tbsp.)

Orange Brûlé
(made with yogurt)

Number of Daily Servings Provided

Fats, Oils & Sweets ●		
Milk, Yogurt & Cheese	½	Meat, Poultry & Fish
Vegetable	2 ½	Fruit
Bread, Cereal,	2	Rice & Pasta

Menu 22

▲ **Spicy Beef with Peppers & Oranges**

Chinese Noodles (½ cup)

Steamed Snow Pea Pods (½ cup)

Almond Cookie

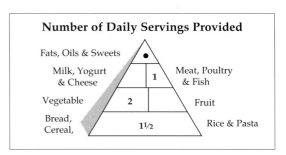

Number of Daily Servings Provided

Fats, Oils & Sweets ●		
Milk, Yogurt & Cheese	1	Meat, Poultry & Fish
Vegetable	2	Fruit
Bread, Cereal,	1½	Rice & Pasta

▲ **Denotes Recipe in Book**

Menu 23

▲ *Turkey Tetrazzini*
2 *Tomato Wedges*
Garlic Bread (1 slice)
▲ *Rhubarb-Blueberry Cobbler*

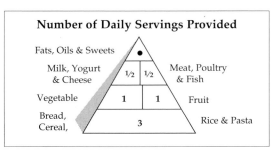

Number of Daily Servings Provided

Fats, Oils & Sweets	●	
Milk, Yogurt & Cheese	1/2	1/2	Meat, Poultry & Fish
Vegetable	1	1	Fruit
Bread, Cereal,	3		Rice & Pasta

Menu 24

▲ *Swordfish with Creole Relish*
▲ *Dixie Vegetable Dish*
Corn Bread (1 piece)
(from mix)
Lemon Sorbet (1/2 cup)

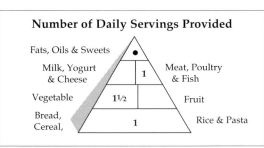

Number of Daily Servings Provided

Fats, Oils & Sweets	●	
Milk, Yogurt & Cheese	1	Meat, Poultry & Fish
Vegetable	1 1/2	Fruit
Bread, Cereal,	1	Rice & Pasta

▲ **Denotes Recipe in Book**

Menu 25

▲ **Beef Eye Round Steaks with Vegetables**

Dinner Roll

Sliced Strawberries & Bananas (¹/₂ cup)

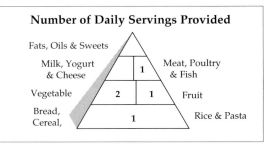

Number of Daily Servings Provided

Fats, Oils & Sweets		
Milk, Yogurt & Cheese	1	Meat, Poultry & Fish
Vegetable	2 1	Fruit
Bread, Cereal,	1	Rice & Pasta

Menu 26

▲ **Taco Salad**

▲ **No-guilt Refried Beans**

Ice Cream Sandwich Cookie
2 basic sugar cookies, ¹/₄ cup low-fat ice cream ◆

Number of Daily Servings Provided

Fats, Oils & Sweets	●	
Milk, Yogurt & Cheese	1¹/₂	Meat, Poultry & Fish
Vegetable	1	Fruit
Bread, Cereal,	1	Rice & Pasta

▲ **Denotes Recipe in Book**   ◆ Look for Healthy Choice® products at your favorite supermarket.

Menu 27

▲ *Scallops with
Wine & Cheese Sauce*

*Steamed Green Beans (½ cup)
with Slivered Almonds (2 tsp.)*

*Cooked Rhubarb
with Sliced Strawberries (½ cup)*

Number of Daily Servings Provided

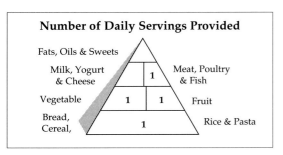

Fats, Oils & Sweets	
Milk, Yogurt & Cheese	1 — Meat, Poultry & Fish
Vegetable	1 — 1 — Fruit
Bread, Cereal,	1 — Rice & Pasta

Menu 28

▲ *Chicken Marengo*

Spinach Linguine (½ cup)

Crisp Green Salad
½ cup lettuce, ½ cup sliced cucumber,
¼ cup red and yellow pepper strips,
1 tbsp. light Italian dressing

Fresh Raspberries (½ cup)

Number of Daily Servings Provided

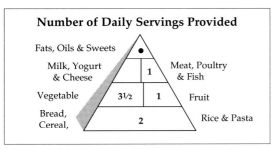

Fats, Oils & Sweets	●
Milk, Yogurt & Cheese	1 — Meat, Poultry & Fish
Vegetable	3½ — 1 — Fruit
Bread, Cereal,	2 — Rice & Pasta

▲ **Denotes Recipe in Book**

Menu 29

▲ *South of the Border Muffuletta*
▲ *Colorful Marinated Vegetables*
Watermelon (2 wedges)

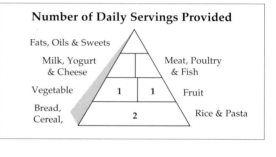

Number of Daily Servings Provided

Fats, Oils & Sweets

Milk, Yogurt & Cheese — Meat, Poultry & Fish

Vegetable **1** | **1** Fruit

Bread, Cereal, — **2** — Rice & Pasta

Menu 30

▲ *Plum-sauced Pork Medallions*
▲ *Spaetzle*
Steamed Sliced Zucchini (½ cup)
Gingerbread (1 piece)
(from mix)

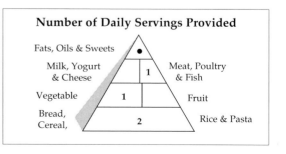

Number of Daily Servings Provided

Fats, Oils & Sweets ●

Milk, Yogurt & Cheese **1** Meat, Poultry & Fish

Vegetable **1** Fruit

Bread, Cereal, — **2** — Rice & Pasta

▲ **Denotes Recipe in Book**

Menu 31

▲ **Lemon Thyme Chicken with Vegetables**

Orzo Pasta (½ cup) with Slivered Sun-dried Tomatoes (2 tsp.)

▲ **Crunchy Coffee Frozen Torte**

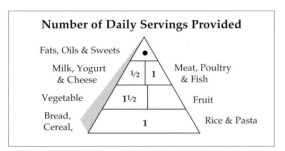

Number of Daily Servings Provided

Fats, Oils & Sweets ●

Milk, Yogurt & Cheese — ½ 1 — Meat, Poultry & Fish

Vegetable — 1½ — Fruit

Bread, Cereal, — 1 — Rice & Pasta

Menu 32

▲ **Chinese-style Fish with Vegetables**

White Rice (½ cup)

Wilted Spinach Salad
1 cup spinach, ¼ cup red onion strips, 1 tbsp. red wine vinegar dressing, freshly ground pepper

Peach Sorbet (½ cup)

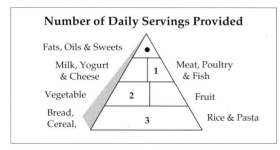

Number of Daily Servings Provided

Fats, Oils & Sweets ●

Milk, Yogurt & Cheese — 1 — Meat, Poultry & Fish

Vegetable — 2 — Fruit

Bread, Cereal, — 3 — Rice & Pasta

▲ **Denotes Recipe in Card Series**

Menu 33

▲ **Broiled Fruited Pork Chops**

**Steamed French-cut
Green Beans (1/2 cup)**

Oven-fried Potato Wedges (5 oz.)

▲ **Apricot Bread**

Number of Daily Servings Provided

Fats, Oils & Sweets ●

Milk, Yogurt & Cheese — 1 — Meat, Poultry & Fish

Vegetable — 2 — 1 — Fruit

Bread, Cereal, — 1 — Rice & Pasta

Menu 34

▲ **Turkey-stuffed Cabbage Rolls**

Corn on the Cob

▲ **Raspberry Pie**

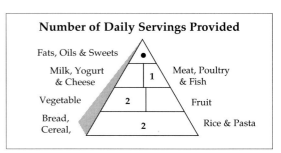

Number of Daily Servings Provided

Fats, Oils & Sweets ●

Milk, Yogurt & Cheese — 1 — Meat, Poultry & Fish

Vegetable — 2 — Fruit

Bread, Cereal, — 2 — Rice & Pasta

▲ **Denotes Recipe in Book**

Menu 35

Grilled Turkey Steak (4 oz.)

▲ *Pasta with Onion Sauce*

▲ *Spinach & Shallot Dressing
on Mixed Greens*

Sliced Fresh Pear

Number of Daily Servings Provided

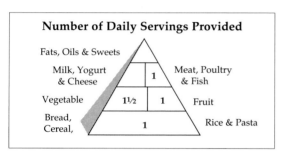

Fats, Oils & Sweets

Milk, Yogurt & Cheese — **1** — Meat, Poultry & Fish

Vegetable — **1½** — **1** — Fruit

Bread, Cereal, — **1** — Rice & Pasta

Menu 36

▲ *Spicy Manhattan Clam Chowder*

Crusty Sourdough Roll

*Fruit Bowl (½ cup)
with Vanilla Yogurt (2 tbsp.)*

Number of Daily Servings Provided

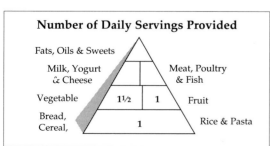

Fats, Oils & Sweets

Milk, Yogurt & Cheese — Meat, Poultry & Fish

Vegetable — **1½** — **1** — Fruit

Bread, Cereal, — **1** — Rice & Pasta

▲ **Denotes Recipe in Book**

APPETIZERS, SNACKS & BEVERAGES

CRAB & CHEESE BUNDLES

2 tablespoons sliced green onion
2 tablespoons finely chopped green pepper
½ cup flaked crabmeat
½ cup nonfat or light ricotta cheese
1 teaspoon Dijon mustard
⅛ teaspoon freshly ground pepper
3 sheets frozen phyllo dough
    (18 x 14-inch sheets), defrosted
1 tablespoon margarine or butter, melted

8 servings

1 Heat oven to 400°F. Spray large baking sheet with nonstick vegetable cooking spray. Set aside.

2 Combine onion, green pepper, crabmeat, cheese, mustard and pepper in medium mixing bowl. Set filling aside.

3 Place 1 sheet phyllo on flat work surface. (Keep remaining sheets covered with plastic wrap.) Quickly brush sheet with one-third of margarine. Lay second sheet of phyllo over first. Brush with half of remaining margarine. Lay third sheet over second. Brush with remaining margarine.

4 Cut layered sheets lengthwise into quarters, then crosswise into quarters, making 16 pieces. Put about 2 teaspoons filling in center of each.

5 Shape each phyllo piece around filling like money bag. Place phyllo bundles on prepared baking sheet. Bake for 14 to 16 minutes, or until golden brown. Serve warm.

Microwave tip: For less crisp vegetables, combine onion and green pepper in 1-cup measure. Cover with plastic wrap. Microwave at High for 1 to 2 minutes, or until vegetables are tender-crisp, stirring once. Continue as directed.

Nutrition Facts

Serving Size 2 bundles (36g)
Servings per Recipe 8
Calories 70
Calories from Fat 30

Amount/serving	%DV*	Amount/serving	%DV*
Total Fat 3g	5%	Total Carbohydrate 5g	2%
Saturated Fat 1g	5%	Dietary Fiber 0g	<1%
Cholesterol 13mg	4%	Sugars 0g	
Sodium 99mg	4%	Protein 4g	

Vitamin A 2% • Vitamin C 4% • Calcium 8% • Iron 2%
*Percent Daily Values (DV) are based on a 2000 calorie diet.

Menu Planning Guide
One serving of this recipe provides:

Diet Exchanges:
1 lean meat

46

MUSTARD-DILL CHICKEN STRIPS

3 tablespoons sugar

2 tablespoons all-purpose flour

½ teaspoon dried dill weed

¼ teaspoon salt

1 cup skim milk

¼ cup white vinegar

3 tablespoons frozen cholesterol-free
     egg product ◆, defrosted, or 1 egg yolk

3 tablespoons Dijon mustard

2 boneless whole chicken breasts (8 to 10 oz. each),
     split in half, skin removed, cut into ¾-inch
     strips
     Fresh dill weed sprigs

6 servings

1 Combine sugar, flour, dried dill weed and salt in 1-quart saucepan. Blend in milk, vinegar, egg product and mustard. Cook over medium heat for 7 to 15 minutes, or until sauce thickens and bubbles, stirring constantly with whisk. Cool slightly.

2 Arrange chicken in even layer in shallow baking dish. Pour ¾ cup sauce over chicken. Cover remaining sauce with plastic wrap. Chill. Stir chicken to coat with sauce. Cover with plastic wrap. Chill at least 1 hour.

3 Drain and discard sauce from chicken. Arrange chicken on rack in broiler pan. Place under conventional broiler with surface of chicken 7 inches from heat. Broil for 10 to 15 minutes, or until meat is no longer pink, turning and brushing frequently with ¼ cup reserved sauce.

4 Place chicken on serving plate. Top each strip with some of remaining sauce and a fresh dill sprig. Serve with remaining sauce.

Microwave tip: In medium mixing bowl, combine sugar, flour, dried dill weed and salt. Blend in milk, vinegar, egg product and mustard. Microwave at High for 3 to 4 minutes, or until sauce thickens and bubbles, stirring every minute. Continue as directed.

◆ Look for Healthy Choice® products at your favorite supermarket.

Nutrition Facts	Amount/serving	%DV*	Amount/serving	%DV*
Serving Size 3-4 oz. (65g) Servings per Recipe 6 Calories 94 Calories from Fat 18	Total Fat 2g	3%	Total Carbohydrate 3g	1%
	Saturated Fat <1g	3%	Dietary Fiber <1g	0%
	Cholesterol 40mg	13%	Sugars 2g	
	Sodium 90mg	14%	Protein 15g	

Vitamin A 2% • Vitamin C 0% • Calcium 2% • Iron 4%

*Percent Daily Values (DV) are based on a 2000 calorie diet.

Menu Planning Guide

One serving of this recipe provides:

1 Meat, Poultry & Fish

Diet Exchanges:

2 lean meat

TROPICAL FRUIT PUNCH & ICE RING

2 cups crushed ice
1 can (20 oz.) pineapple tidbits in juice, drained
    (reserve juice)
15 maraschino cherries with stems
7 slices lime (1/4 inch thick)
1 bottle (64 oz.) tropical fruit juice
    (pine-orange-guava or pine-passion-banana),
    chilled, divided
1 can (10 oz.) frozen piña colada drink mixer
    concentrate, defrosted, divided
1 bottle (33.8 oz.) ginger ale, chilled

18 servings

1 Combine ice and pineapple in medium mixing bowl. Spoon ice mixture into 6½-cup ring mold. Arrange cherries and lime slices over ice mixture.

2 Combine 1½ cups fruit juice and ½ cup concentrate in 4-cup measure. Pour over fruit. Freeze mold at least 8 hours or overnight.

3 Combine remaining fruit juice, remaining concentrate, reserved pineapple juice and the ginger ale in punch bowl. Dip mold into warm water for 10 to 15 seconds. Carefully unmold ice ring and place fruit-side-up in punch bowl.

Nutrition Facts	Amount/serving	%DV*	Amount/serving	%DV*	Menu Planning Guide
Serving Size 3/4 cup (221g)	Total Fat <1g	1%	Total Carbohydrate 25g	8%	One serving of this recipe provides: 1½ Fruit
	Saturated Fat <1g	1%	Dietary Fiber <1g	2%	
Servings per Recipe 18	Cholesterol 0mg	0%	Sugars 25g		
Calories 104 Calories from Fat 4	Sodium 12mg	0%	Protein <1g		

Vitamin A 25% • Vitamin C 40% • Calcium 2% • Iron 4%
*Percent Daily Values (DV) are based on a 2000 calorie diet.

Diet Exchanges:
1½ fruit

STUFFED CHERRY TOMATOES

24 cherry tomatoes (about 1 pint)
½ cup plain yogurt cheese*
 3 tablespoons light or nonfat cream cheese ◆, softened
½ teaspoon dried dill weed
¼ teaspoon dry mustard
⅛ teaspoon onion powder

Finely chopped pecans (optional)
Shredded fresh Parmesan cheese (optional)

8 servings

1 Cut off tops of tomatoes. Scoop out and discard pulp. Set shells aside.

2 Combine cheeses in small mixing bowl. Stir in dill weed, mustard and onion powder.

3 Spoon or pipe mixture evenly into tomato shells (about 1 teaspoon each). Sprinkle tops with pecans or Parmesan cheese. Chill.

*Yogurt Cheese:

1 carton (16 oz.) plain nonfat or low-fat yogurt (no added gelatin)

Yield: 1 cup

Line mesh strainer with 3 paper towels. Place strainer over bowl. Spoon yogurt into prepared strainer. Cover with plastic wrap. Let drain overnight in refrigerator. Discard liquid. Store cheese in sealed container. Use yogurt cheese instead of sour cream or cream cheese in recipes.

◆ Look for Healthy Choice® products at your favorite supermarket.

Nutrition Facts	Amount/serving	%DV*	Amount/serving	%DV*
Serving Size 3 tomatoes (72g)	Total Fat 1g	2%	Total Carbohydrate 4g	1%
Servings per Recipe 8	Saturated Fat <1g	3%	Dietary Fiber <1g	2%
Calories 33	Cholesterol 3mg	1%	Sugars 3g	
Calories from Fat 11	Sodium 33mg	1%	Protein 2g	
	Vitamin A 4% • Vitamin C 15% • Calcium 4% • Iron 2%			
	*Percent Daily Values (DV) are based on a 2000 calorie diet.			

Menu Planning Guide
One serving of this recipe provides:
½ Vegetable

Diet Exchanges:
½ vegetable

FRESH VEGETABLE CRISP

2 flour tortillas (8-inch)
1 pkg. (3 oz.) nonfat or low-fat cream cheese ◆,
    softened
¼ cup plus 2 tablespoons shredded low-fat
    Cheddar cheese, divided
½ teaspoon dried basil leaves

Dash garlic powder
4 cups water
1 cup small fresh broccoli flowerets
½ cup sliced fresh mushrooms
3 thin red pepper rings

6 servings

1 Heat 10-inch nonstick skillet over medium heat. Spray 1 tortilla lightly on both sides with nonstick vegetable cooking spray. Place in skillet. Cook for 2½ to 3½ minutes, or until tortilla just begins to brown, turning over once. Place tortilla between 2 paper towels. Repeat with remaining tortilla. Set aside.

2 Heat oven to 350°F. In small mixing bowl, combine cream cheese, 2 tablespoons Cheddar cheese, the basil and garlic powder. Spread mixture evenly on 1 tortilla. Top with remaining tortilla. Place on baking sheet. Set aside. In 2-quart saucepan, bring water to boil over high heat.

3 Immerse broccoli in water for 1 minute, or until color brightens. Remove with slotted spoon. Plunge broccoli immediately into ice water. Drain. Arrange broccoli, mushrooms and pepper rings on top tortilla. Sprinkle evenly with remaining ¼ cup Cheddar cheese. Bake for 7 to 9 minutes, or until vegetable crisp is hot and cheese melts. Cut into wedges to serve.

Microwave tip: Place 1 tortilla on paper-towel-lined plate. Microwave at High for 1¾ to 2¼ minutes, or just until surface is dry and puffy, rotating plate once. Place tortilla on cooling rack to cool and crisp. Repeat with remaining tortilla. Continue as directed.

◆ Look for Healthy Choice® products at your favorite supermarket.

Nutrition Facts	Amount/serving	%DV*	Amount/serving	%DV*
Serving Size 1 slice (59g)	Total Fat 2g	3%	Total Carbohydrate 9g	3%
Servings per Recipe 6	Saturated Fat <1g	4%	Dietary Fiber 1g	4%
Calories 78	Cholesterol 7mg	2%	Sugars <1g	
Calories from Fat 20	Sodium 201mg	8%	Protein 6g	

Vitamin A 10% • Vitamin C 40% • Calcium 8% • Iron 4%
*Percent Daily Values (DV) are based on a 2000 calorie diet.

Menu Planning Guide
One serving of this recipe provides:
½ Vegetable
½ Bread, Cereal, Rice & Pasta

Diet Exchanges:
½ starch • ½ vegetable

WASSAIL*

1 medium seedless orange
24 whole cloves
2 cups red wine
2 cups apple cider
¼ cup sugar
2 teaspoons grated lemon peel
2 slices peeled fresh gingerroot
1 small stick cinnamon

¼ teaspoon ground nutmeg
¼ teaspoon ground allspice

6 servings

* Wassail is from the Norse ves heill meaning "be in good health." It is a slightly bitter drink made with ale or wine, sweetened with sugar and flavored with spices.

1 Cut orange into 8 wedges. Insert 3 cloves into rind of each wedge. Set aside.

2 Combine remaining ingredients in 3-quart saucepan. Stir until sugar is dissolved. Add orange wedges. Bring mixture to simmer over medium heat, stirring occasionally. (Do not boil.) Reduce heat to medium-low. Simmer wassail for 10 minutes to blend flavors.

Tip: If desired, place peel, gingerroot and remaining spices in cheesecloth bag before adding to wassail.

Nutrition Facts

Serving Size approximately ⅔ cup (194g)
Servings per Recipe 6
Calories 140
Calories from Fat 0

Amount/serving	%DV*	Amount/serving	%DV*
Total Fat 0g	0%	Total Carbohydrate 23g	8%
Saturated Fat 0g	0%	Dietary Fiber 1g	4%
Cholesterol 0mg	0%	Sugars 21g	
Sodium 5mg	0%	Protein 0g	

Vitamin A 0% • Vitamin C 20% • Calcium 2% • Iron 4%

*Percent Daily Values (DV) are based on a 2000 calorie diet.

Menu Planning Guide
One serving of this recipe provides:
1 Fruit

Diet Exchanges:
½ starch • 1 fruit • 1 fat

BASIL & CREAM CHEESE SPREAD

¼ cup chopped walnuts (optional)
1 pkg. (8 oz.) low-fat cream cheese, softened
2 tablespoons snipped fresh basil
2 cloves garlic, minced
½ teaspoon grated lemon peel
2 medium zucchini, thinly sliced (2 cups)

20 servings

Serving suggestion: Serve with crackers or raw vegetables.

1 Heat oven to 350°F. In 8-inch square baking pan, bake walnuts for 5 to 7 minutes, or just until nuts begin to brown, stirring once or twice. Set aside.

2 Combine cream cheese, basil, garlic and peel in small mixing bowl. Stir in walnuts. Cover with plastic wrap. Chill 1 to 2 hours to blend flavors. If desired, garnish with additional chopped walnuts. Serve with zucchini slices.

Nutrition Facts	Amount/serving	%DV*	Amount/serving	%DV*
Serving Size 1 tablespoon (25g)	Total Fat 2g	3%	Total Carbohydrate 1g	0%
	Saturated Fat 1g	7%	Dietary Fiber <1g	0%
Servings per Recipe 20	Cholesterol 6mg	2%	Sugars 1g	
	Sodium 34mg	1%	Protein 1g	
Calories 29 Calories from Fat 18	Vitamin A 2% • Vitamin C 2% • Calcium 2% • Iron 2%			

*Percent Daily Values (DV) are based on a 2000 calorie diet.

Menu Planning Guide
One serving of this recipe provides:

Diet Exchanges:
½ fat

OLD-FASHIONED RASPBERRY SODA

1 pkg. (16 oz.) frozen unsweetened raspberries

¼ cup sugar

2 tablespoons fresh lemon juice

2 tablespoons Triple Sec or orange juice

12 scoops low-fat vanilla ice cream ◆

12 cups carbonated water, lemon-lime soda,
    champagne or spumanti, chilled

12 servings

*Strawberry Soda: Follow recipe, except substitute
1 pkg. (16 oz.) frozen unsweetened strawberries
for raspberries.*

Black Raspberry Soda: Follow recipe, except substitute 1 pkg. (10 oz.) frozen unsweetened black raspberries for raspberries.

1 Combine raspberries, sugar, lemon juice and Triple Sec in 2-quart saucepan. Cook over medium heat for 7 to 10 minutes, or until raspberries are defrosted and sugar is dissolved, stirring occasionally.

2 Process raspberry mixture in food processor or blender until smooth. Strain through fine-mesh sieve into 4-cup measure. Discard seeds.

3 Place 2 tablespoons raspberry mixture and 1 scoop ice cream in 12-oz. glass. Add 1 cup carbonated water. Repeat with remaining mixture, ice cream and carbonated water.

Microwave tip: Combine raspberries, sugar, lemon juice and Triple Sec in 2-quart casserole. Cover. Microwave at High for 5 to 7 minutes, or until raspberries are defrosted and sugar is dissolved, stirring once. Continue as directed.

◆ Look for Healthy Choice® products at your favorite supermarket.

Nutrition Facts	Amount/serving	%DV*	Amount/serving	%DV*
Serving Size 1 soda (133g) Servings per Recipe 12 Calories 164 Calories from Fat 20	Total Fat 2g	3%	Total Carbohydrate 31g	10%
	Saturated Fat 1g	5%	Dietary Fiber 2g	8%
	Cholesterol 5mg	2%	Sugars 24g	
	Sodium 64mg	3%	Protein 4g	

Vitamin A 0% • Vitamin C 20% • Calcium 15% • Iron 2%
*Percent Daily Values (DV) are based on a 2000 calorie diet.

Menu Planning Guide
One serving of this recipe provides:
½ Fruit

Diet Exchanges:
1 starch • ½ fruit • ½ fat

SOUPS, SALADS & SANDWICHES

SOUTHERN SUCCOTASH SOUP

1 cup dried black-eyed peas
½ cup dried lima beans
½ cup dried red kidney beans
10 cups water, divided
1 tablespoon olive oil
2 medium carrots, sliced (1 cup)
2 stalks celery, sliced (1 cup)
1 medium onion, sliced (1 cup)
3-lb. whole broiler-fryer chicken, cut into 8 pieces,
    skin removed
    Cajun Seasoning Mix*
2 cups frozen corn
1 pkg. (9 oz.) frozen lima beans

14 servings

*Cajun Seasoning Mix
1 tablespoon dried parsley flakes
1½ teaspoons dried oregano leaves
1½ teaspoons dried thyme leaves
1 teaspoon paprika
1 tablespoon instant chicken bouillon granules
1 teaspoon ground cumin
½ teaspoon instant minced garlic
½ teaspoon freshly ground pepper
¼ to ½ teaspoon cayenne
1 teaspoon salt

In small bowl, combine all ingredients.

1 Rinse and drain dried peas and beans; remove any grit and discolored or shriveled legumes. Place in 3-quart saucepan. Add 4 cups water. Bring to boil over medium-high heat, stirring occasionally. Boil for 2 minutes. Cover. Remove from heat. Let stand for 1 hour. Drain and discard liquid from peas and beans. Rinse with warm water. Drain. Set aside.

2 Place oil in 6-quart Dutch oven or stockpot. Heat over medium-high heat. Add carrots, celery and onion. Cook for 4 to 5 minutes, or until vegetables are tender, stirring frequently.

3 Reduce heat to medium. Stir in prepared peas and beans, the chicken, seasoning mix and remaining 6 cups water. Bring mixture to boil, stirring frequently. Reduce heat to low and simmer, partially covered, for 1½ hours, stirring occasionally.

4 Remove chicken from soup. Cool slightly. Cut meat from bones. Discard bones. Add chicken, corn and frozen lima beans to soup. Continue to cook, partially covered, for 30 to 45 minutes, or until beans are softened and soup is hot, stirring occasionally.

Nutrition Facts	Amount/serving	%DV*	Amount/serving	%DV*
Serving Size 1 cup (25g)	Total Fat 4g	7%	Total Carbohydrate 28g	9%
Servings per Recipe 14	Saturated Fat 1g	5%	Dietary Fiber 6g	25%
Calories 200	Cholesterol 30mg	9%	Sugars 4g	
Calories from Fat 40	Sodium 206mg	9%	Protein 16g	

Vitamin A 30% • Vitamin C 6% • Calcium 8% • Iron 15%
*Percent Daily Values (DV) are based on a 2000 calorie diet.

Menu Planning Guide
One serving of this recipe provides:

1 Meat, Poultry, & Fish
½ Vegetable

Diet Exchanges:
1 lean meat • 2 starch

FRUITED COUSCOUS SALAD

1½ cups hot water

¼ teaspoon salt

1 cup uncooked couscous*

½ cup frozen orange juice concentrate, defrosted

2 tablespoons white wine vinegar

1 tablespoon sugar

1 tablespoon vegetable oil

1 teaspoon grated orange peel

1 cup fresh blueberries

1 cup fresh raspberries

1 cup fresh strawberries, hulled and cut in half

1 fresh peach, pitted and cut into ½-inch chunks

1 fresh plum, pitted and cut into ½-inch chunks

¼ cup fresh mint leaves

12 servings

Couscous is a Middle-Eastern pasta available in specialty markets and large supermarkets.

1 Combine water and salt in 2-quart saucepan. Bring to boil over medium-high heat. Stir in couscous. Cover. Remove from heat. Let stand for 5 minutes. Fluff couscous lightly with fork. Place in medium mixing bowl. Set aside.

2 Combine concentrate, vinegar, sugar, oil and peel in 2-cup measure. Blend well with whisk. Add half of juice mixture to couscous. Mix well. Cover and chill at least 1 hour.

3 Add remaining juice mixture and remaining ingredients to couscous mixture. Toss gently to combine. Line serving bowl with lettuce, if desired.

Nutrition Facts	Amount/serving	%DV*	Amount/serving	%DV*
Serving Size 1 cup (123g)	Total Fat 2g	2%	Total Carbohydrate 25g	8%
Servings per Recipe 12	Saturated Fat <1g	1%	Dietary Fiber 3g	10%
Calories 122	Cholesterol 0mg	0%	Sugars 9g	
Calories from Fat 14	Sodium 4mg	0%	Protein 3g	

Vitamin A 2% • Vitamin C 50% • Calcium 2% • Iron 2%
*Percent Daily Values (DV) are based on a 2000 calorie diet.

Menu Planning Guide
One serving of this recipe provides:
½ Fruit
1 Bread, Cereal, Rice & Pasta

Diet Exchanges:
1½ starch • ½ fruit

HERBED FLANK STEAK SANDWICHES

1   tablespoon vegetable oil
⅓   cup chopped onion
1   clove garlic, minced
⅓   cup red wine vinegar
2   tablespoons packed brown sugar
1   tablespoon snipped fresh parsley
1   tablespoon snipped fresh oregano leaves
1   tablespoon fresh thyme leaves
1 - lb. well-trimmed beef flank steak
4   kaiser rolls, split

Sweet hot mustard
8   slices tomato
Lettuce leaves

4 servings

1 Place oil in 1-quart saucepan. Heat over medium-low heat. Add onion and garlic. Cook for 3 to 4 minutes, or until onion is tender, stirring occasionally. Add vinegar, sugar, parsley, oregano and thyme. Mix well. Set aside to cool.

2 Score steak with 6 diagonal slashes, about ⅛ inch deep. Place steak in large plastic food-storage bag. Add marinade. Secure bag. Turn to coat. Chill 6 hours or overnight, turning bag occasionally.

3 Spray cooking grid with nonstick vegetable cooking spray. Prepare grill for medium direct heat. Drain and discard marinade from meat. Place steak on cooking grid. Grill, covered, for 12 to 14 minutes, or until desired doneness, turning over once.

4 Carve steak across grain into thin slices. Spread cut sides of each roll with mustard. Top evenly with steak, tomato and lettuce.

Microwave tip: In 2-cup measure, combine oil, onion and garlic. Cover with plastic wrap. Microwave at High for 2 to 3 minutes, or until onion is tender, stirring once. Continue as directed.

Nutrition Facts	Amount/serving	%DV*	Amount/serving	%DV*
Serving Size 1 sandwich (188g)	Total Fat 13g	20%	Total Carbohydrate 32g	11%
Servings per Recipe 4	Saturated Fat 4g	19%	Dietary Fiber 1g	4%
Calories 360	Cholesterol 57mg	19%	Sugars 3g	
Calories from Fat 110	Sodium 413mg	17%	Protein 29g	

Vitamin A 2% • Vitamin C 15% • Calcium 2% • Iron 30%
*Percent Daily Values (DV) are based on a 2000 calorie diet.

Menu Planning Guide
One serving of this recipe provides:
1   Meat, Poultry & Fish
2   Bread, Cereal, Rice & Pasta

Diet Exchanges:
3 lean meat • 1 starch

HEARTY MINESTRONE SOUP

1/3 cup pesto, divided

1/2 lb. beef stew meat, cut into 1/2-inch pieces

2 medium carrots, sliced (1 cup)

2 stalks celery, chopped (1 cup)

1 medium onion, chopped (1 cup)

4 oz. fresh green beans, cut into 2-inch lengths
    (1 cup)

8 cups water

1/4 cup dehydrated vegetable flakes

1 tablespoon instant chicken bouillon granules

1 can (28 oz.) whole tomatoes, drained and cut up

1 can (16 oz.) red kidney beans, rinsed and drained

1 1/2 cups uncooked rainbow rotini

1 cup uncooked bow-tie pasta

1 medium zucchini, sliced (1 cup)

1/2 cup uncooked macaroni rings

12 servings

1 Heat 1 tablespoon pesto over medium-high heat in 6-quart Dutch oven or stockpot. Add stew meat. Cook for 4 to 5 minutes, or until meat is browned, stirring frequently. Add carrots, celery, onion and beans. Cook for 3 to 5 minutes, or until onions are tender, stirring frequently.

2 Add water, remaining pesto, the vegetable flakes and bouillon. Bring mixture to boil over medium heat, stirring frequently. Reduce heat to low. Simmer, partially covered, for 45 minutes to 1 hour, or until meat is tender, stirring occasionally.

3 Return mixture to boil over medium heat. Add remaining ingredients. Reduce heat to low. Simmer for 15 to 20 minutes, or until pasta is tender and soup is hot, stirring occasionally.

Nutrition Facts	Amount/serving	%DV*	Amount/serving	%DV*
Serving Size 1 cup (374g)	Total Fat 7g	10%	Total Carbohydrate 28g	9%
Servings per Recipe 12	Saturated Fat 2g	10%	Dietary Fiber 5g	20%
Calories 213	Cholesterol 17mg	5%	Sugars 6g	
Calories from Fat 61	Sodium 502mg	21%	Protein 11g	

Vitamin A 40% • Vitamin C 25% • Calcium 10% • Iron 15%
*Percent Daily Values (DV) are based on a 2000 calorie diet.

Menu Planning Guide
One serving of this recipe provides:
1/2 Meat, Poultry & Fish
1 Vegetable
1/2 Bread, Cereal, Rice & Pasta

Diet Exchanges:
1/2 medium-fat meat • 1 1/2 starch • 1 vegetable

WARM NEW POTATO SALAD

1 lb. new potatoes, cut into quarters (3 cups)
¾ cup water
2 cups frozen broccoli, green beans, pearl onions
    and red pepper vegetable mixture
⅓ cup plain nonfat or low-fat yogurt
1 tablespoon snipped fresh Italian parsley
    or cilantro leaves
1 tablespoon Dijon mustard
⅛ teaspoon salt

6 servings

1 Combine potatoes and water in 2-quart saucepan. Bring to boil over high heat. Cover. Reduce heat to low. Simmer for 15 to 20 minutes, or until potatoes are tender-crisp.

2 Stir in vegetable mixture. Re-cover. Increase heat to medium-high. Cook for 4 to 5 minutes, or until potatoes are tender and vegetables are hot, stirring occasionally. Drain. Set aside.

3 Combine remaining ingredients in serving bowl. Add potato mixture. Toss gently to coat. Serve warm.

Microwave tip: Decrease water to 2 tablespoons. In 2-quart casserole, combine potatoes and water. Cover. Microwave at High for 6 to 11 minutes, or until potatoes are tender-crisp, stirring once. Stir in vegetable mixture. Re-cover. Microwave at High for 4 to 7 minutes, or until potatoes are tender and vegetables are hot, stirring once or twice. Continue as directed.

Nutrition Facts

Serving Size approximately ½ cup (164g)
Servings per Recipe 6
Calories 85
Calories from Fat 3

Amount/serving	%DV*	Amount/serving	%DV*
Total Fat <1g	0%	Total Carbohydrate 18g	6%
Saturated Fat <1g	0%	Dietary Fiber 3g	10%
Cholesterol <1mg	0%	Sugars 3g	
Sodium 113mg	5%	Protein 3g	

Vitamin A 6% • Vitamin C 40% • Calcium 6% • Iron 4%

*Percent Daily Values (DV) are based on a 2000 calorie diet.

Menu Planning Guide

One serving of this recipe provides:
1 Vegetable

Diet Exchanges:

1 starch • ½ vegetable

GREEK BURGERS

¾ cup water

¼ cup uncooked bulgur (cracked wheat)

¼ cup plain nonfat or low-fat yogurt

½ teaspoon dried dill weed

1 cup finely chopped seeded cucumber

1 lb. lean ground beef ◆, crumbled

½ to 1 teaspoon grated lemon peel

½ teaspoon dried oregano leaves

½ teaspoon salt

¼ teaspoon pepper

6 pita loaves (6-inch), warmed
  Leaf lettuce

12 slices tomato

6 servings

1 Bring water to boil over high heat in 1-quart saucepan. Remove from heat. Stir in bulgur. Cover. Let stand for 30 minutes, or until bulgur softens. Meanwhile, in small mixing bowl, combine yogurt, dill weed and cucumber. Cover with plastic wrap. Chill.

2 Combine beef, peel, oregano, salt and pepper in medium mixing bowl. Drain any excess water from bulgur. Add bulgur to beef mixture. Mix well.

3 Form mixture into six ¾-inch-thick oval patties. Place on rack in broiler pan. Place under broiler with surface of meat 4 inches from heat. Broil burgers 8 to 10 minutes, or until desired doneness, turning burgers over once.

4 Fold each pita loaf in half. Place lettuce, 1 burger and 2 tomato slices in each pita. Spoon cucumber mixture evenly into each pita. Secure with wooden pick.

Microwave tip: To warm pita loaves, layer them between 2 dampened paper towels. Microwave at High for 1 to 2 minutes, or just until pitas are warm to the touch.

◆ Look for Healthy Choice® products at your favorite supermarket.

Nutrition Facts	Amount/serving	%DV*	Amount/serving	%DV*
Serving Size 1 burger (180g)	Total Fat 11g	17%	Total Carbohydrate 36g	12%
Servings per Recipe 6	Saturated Fat 4g	20%	Dietary Fiber 1g	6%
Calories 337	Cholesterol 58mg	19%	Sugars 2g	
Calories from Fat 97	Sodium 559mg	23%	Protein 22g	

Vitamin A 0% • Vitamin C 2% • Calcium 8% • Iron 20%
*Percent Daily Values (DV) are based on a 2000 calorie diet.

Menu Planning Guide
One serving of this recipe provides:
1 Meat, Poultry & Fish
2 Bread, Cereal, Rice & Pasta

Diet Exchanges:
2 medium-fat meat • 2 starch

MEXICAN CORN CHOWDER

1 small onion, chopped (½ cup)

⅓ cup chopped green pepper

1 clove garlic, minced

1 can (10¾ oz.) condensed chicken broth

1 pkg. (10 oz.) frozen corn

1 medium tomato, seeded and chopped (1 cup)

1 cup water

2 tablespoons canned chopped green chilies

1 teaspoon dried parsley flakes

¼ teaspoon salt

¼ teaspoon ground cumin

⅛ teaspoon chili powder

4 servings

1 Spray 2-quart saucepan with nonstick vegetable cooking spray. Add onion, pepper and garlic. Cook over medium heat for 5 to 7 minutes, or until vegetables are tender, stirring frequently. (If vegetables begin to stick, move them to one side and spray saucepan with nonstick vegetable cooking spray.)

2 Stir in remaining ingredients. Bring to boil over high heat. Reduce heat to low and simmer, covered, for 6 to 10 minutes, or until chowder is hot and flavors are blended, stirring occasionally.

Microwave tip: In 2-quart casserole, combine onion, pepper and garlic. Cover. Microwave at High for 5 to 7 minutes, or until vegetables are tender, stirring once or twice. Stir in remaining ingredients. Re-cover. Microwave at High for 8 to 12 minutes, or until chowder is hot and flavors are blended, stirring once or twice.

Nutrition Facts

Serving Size 1 cup (281g)
Servings per Recipe 4
Calories 93
Calories from Fat 6

Amount/serving	%DV*	Amount/serving	%DV*
Total Fat 1g	1%	Total Carbohydrate 20g	7%
Saturated Fat <1g	0%	Dietary Fiber 3g	12%
Cholesterol 0mg	0%	Sugars 4g	
Sodium 393mg	16%	Protein 4g	
Vitamin A 10% • Vitamin C 30% • Calcium 2% • Iron 6%			

*Percent Daily Values (DV) are based on a 2000 calorie diet.

Menu Planning Guide

One serving of this recipe provides:
2 Vegetable

Diet Exchanges:

1 starch • 1 vegetable

HOT & SPICY PORK SALAD

2 tablespoons reduced-sodium soy sauce

1 tablespoon Chinese hot chili sauce with garlic

1-lb. well-trimmed pork tenderloin, cut into
    2 x ¼-inch strips

3 cups shredded leaf and Bibb lettuce

1 cup shredded green cabbage

½ cup shredded carrot

½ cup thinly sliced red pepper
    Unsalted peanuts (optional)

4 servings

1 Combine soy sauce and chili sauce in 1-cup measure. In small mixing bowl, combine pork strips and 1 tablespoon soy sauce mixture. Cover with plastic wrap. Chill 30 minutes.

2 Combine lettuce, cabbage, carrot and pepper in large mixing bowl or salad bowl. Toss to combine. Set aside.

3 Spray 10-inch nonstick skillet with nonstick vegetable cooking spray. Add pork. Cook over medium heat for 5 to 7 minutes, or just until meat is no longer pink, stirring occasionally. Drain. Add meat and remaining reserved soy sauce mixture to lettuce mixture. Toss to coat. Sprinkle with peanuts.

Nutrition Facts	Amount/serving	%DV*	Amount/serving	%DV*
Serving Size 1½ cups (188g)	Total Fat 5g	7%	Total Carbohydrate 6g	2%
Servings per Recipe 4	Saturated Fat 2g	8%	Dietary Fiber 2g	8%
Calories 177	Cholesterol 71mg	24%	Sugars 3g	
Calories from Fat 41	Sodium 469mg	20%	Protein 27g	

Vitamin A 110% • Vitamin C 60% • Calcium 4% • Iron 15%
*Percent Daily Values (DV) are based on a 2000 calorie diet.

Menu Planning Guide
One serving of this recipe provides:
1 Meat, Poultry & Fish
1 Vegetable

Diet Exchanges:
3 lean meat • 1 vegetable

BARBECUED CHICKEN SANDWICH

1 boneless whole chicken breast (8 to 10 oz.),
   cut in half, skin removed
1 small onion, sliced (½ cup)
¼ cup chopped green pepper
1 clove garlic, minced
1 teaspoon olive oil
1 can (8 oz.) no-salt-added tomato sauce
3 tablespoons tomato paste

2 tablespoons packed brown sugar
1 tablespoon red wine vinegar
1 tablespoon Worcestershire sauce
½ teaspoon dry mustard
4 drops red pepper sauce
4 whole wheat hamburger buns

4 servings

1 Heat oven to 350°F. Place chicken breast in 8-inch square baking dish. Cover with foil. Bake for 20 to 25 minutes, or until meat is no longer pink and juices run clear. Set aside.

2 Place onion, green pepper, garlic and oil in 10-inch nonstick skillet. Cook over medium heat for 3 to 5 minutes, or until vegetables are tender, stirring frequently. Add remaining ingredients, except chicken and buns. Cook over medium heat for 5 minutes, or until barbecue sauce is slightly thickened and flavors are blended, stirring frequently.

3 Shred chicken. Add to barbecue sauce. Cover. Cook over medium heat for 4 to 5 minutes, or until hot, stirring occasionally. Spoon ½ cup mixture onto each bun.

Microwave tip: Place chicken breast on roasting rack or in 8-inch square baking dish. Cover with wax paper. Microwave at High for 4 to 6 minutes, or until meat is no longer pink and juices run clear, rotating once. Continue as directed.

Nutrition Facts

Serving Size 1 sandwich (199g)
Servings per Recipe 4
Calories 269
Calories from Fat 59

Amount/serving	%DV*	Amount/serving	%DV*
Total Fat 7g	10%	Total Carbohydrate 37g	12%
Saturated Fat 2g	8%	Dietary Fiber 3g	12%
Cholesterol 30mg	10%	Sugars 12g	
Sodium 435mg	18%	Protein 16g	

Vitamin A 20% • Vitamin C 35% • Calcium 10% • Iron 15%
*Percent Daily Values (DV) are based on a 2000 calorie diet.

Menu Planning Guide
One serving of this recipe provides:
½ Meat, Poultry & Fish
1 Vegetable
2 Bread, Cereal, Rice & Pasta

Diet Exchanges:
1 lean meat • 2 starch • 1 vegetable

80

ITALIAN VEGETABLE SOUP

3 cups fresh vegetables, any combination
(broccoli, cauliflower, onions, red and green
peppers, cut into 1-inch pieces; carrots, cut
into 1/4-inch slices; snow pea pods)
2 cloves garlic, minced
1 1/4 cups water, divided
1 can (10 1/2 oz.) condensed beef consommé
1/2 cup dry red wine
1 teaspoon Italian seasoning
2 oz. uncooked capellini (angel hair spaghetti),
broken into 2-inch lengths

4 servings

1 Combine vegetables, garlic and 1/2 cup water in 2-quart saucepan. Cover. Cook over medium heat for 8 to 12 minutes, or until vegetables are tender-crisp, stirring occasionally.

2 Stir in consommé, remaining 3/4 cup water, the wine, Italian seasoning and capellini. Bring to boil over high heat. Reduce heat to medium-low. Simmer, uncovered, for 5 to 10 minutes, or until vegetables and capellini are tender, stirring occasionally.

Nutrition Facts	Amount/serving	%DV*	Amount/serving	%DV*
Serving Size approximately 1 cup (281g)	Total Fat <1g	0%	Total Carbohydrate 21g	7%
	Saturated Fat <1g	0%	Dietary Fiber 3g	12%
Servings per Recipe 4	Cholesterol 0mg	0%	Sugars 5g	
Calories 122 Calories from Fat 3	Sodium 405mg	17%	Protein 9g	

Vitamin A 70% • Vitamin C 90% • Calcium 4% • Iron 8%
*Percent Daily Values (DV) are based on a 2000 calorie diet.

Menu Planning Guide
One serving of this recipe provides:
1 1/2 Vegetable
1 Bread, Cereal, Rice & Pasta

Diet Exchanges:
1 starch • 1 1/2 vegetable

TACO SALAD

½ lb. lean ground beef ◆, crumbled

¼ cup chopped onion

1 teaspoon chili powder

¼ teaspoon ground cumin

¼ teaspoon dried oregano leaves

¼ teaspoon salt

1 can (15½ oz.) kidney beans, rinsed and drained

1 medium tomato, seeded and chopped (1 cup)

1 tablespoon reduced-calorie Russian dressing

4 cups shredded lettuce

½ cup thick and chunky salsa

¼ cup plain nonfat or low-fat yogurt

4 servings

1 Combine beef, onion, chili powder, cumin, oregano and salt in 10-inch nonstick skillet. Cook over medium heat for 5 to 7 minutes, or until beef is no longer pink, stirring occasionally. Remove from heat. Drain. Stir in beans, tomato and dressing.

2 Arrange 1 cup lettuce on each plate. Top each serving with about ¾ cup beef mixture. Spoon 2 tablespoons salsa and 1 tablespoon yogurt over each serving.

◆ Look for Healthy Choice® products at your favorite supermarket.

Nutrition Facts	Amount/serving	%DV*	Amount/serving	%DV*
Serving Size 1 salad (300g)	Total Fat 9g	14%	Total Carbohydrate 30g	10%
Servings per Recipe 4	Saturated Fat 3g	17%	Dietary Fiber 8g	32%
Calories 281	Cholesterol 36mg	12%	Sugars 8g	
Calories from Fat 84	Sodium 347mg	14%	Protein 21g	

Vitamin A 25% • Vitamin C 40% • Calcium 8% • Iron 25%

*Percent Daily Values (DV) are based on a 2000 calorie diet.

Menu Planning Guide
One serving of this recipe provides:
1 Meat, Poultry & Fish
1 Vegetable

Diet Exchanges:
1½ medium-fat meat • 1½ starch • 1 vegetable

SOUTH OF THE BORDER MUFFULETTA

1 loaf (1 lb.) round sourdough bread

¼ cup nonfat yogurt cheese*

1 tablespoon sliced green onion

1 clove garlic, minced

1 teaspoon Dijon mustard

⅛ teaspoon chili powder

⅛ teaspoon ground cumin

⅛ teaspoon ground turmeric

6 slices (0.5 oz. each) fully cooked chicken breast

3 slices (1 oz. each) reduced-fat Monterey Jack cheese

1 can (4 oz.) whole green chilies, drained and sliced in half lengthwise

4 slices tomato
  Leaf lettuce

8 servings

* See recipe on page 52.

1 Cut loaf in half crosswise. Cut circle 1 inch from outer edge of crust. Remove bread from circle to 1-inch depth. Reserve bread for future use. Set halves aside.

2 Combine yogurt cheese, onion, garlic, mustard, chili powder, cumin and turmeric in small mixing bowl. Spread yogurt cheese mixture evenly over inside of top and bottom halves of loaf.

3 Layer 2 chicken slices, 1 cheese slice, half of chilies, 2 tomato slices and lettuce on bottom half of loaf. Repeat layers once. Top with 2 chicken slices and 1 cheese slice. Place top half of loaf over filling. Serve in wedges.

Nutrition Facts	Amount/serving	%DV*	Amount/serving	%DV*
Serving Size 1 wedge (113g)	Total Fat 4g	6%	Total Carbohydrate 32g	11%
Servings per Recipe 8	Saturated Fat 2g	8%	Dietary Fiber 2g	8%
Calories 217	Cholesterol 17mg	6%	Sugars 2g	
Calories from Fat 37	Sodium 464mg	19%	Protein 12g	

Vitamin A 6% • Vitamin C 8% • Calcium 15% • Iron 10%

*Percent Daily Values (DV) are based on a 2000 calorie diet.

Menu Planning Guide
One serving of this recipe provides:
2 Bread, Cereal, Rice & Pasta

Diet Exchanges:
1 lean meat • 2 starch

SPINACH & SHALLOT DRESSING

6 *cups coarsely torn fresh spinach leaves, divided*

¼ *cup finely chopped shallots*

¼ *cup apple jelly*

2 *tablespoons white wine vinegar*

¼ *teaspoon dried tarragon leaves*

⅛ *teaspoon salt*

　Mixed salad greens, torn into bite-size
　　pieces (optional)

　Tomato slices (optional)

12 servings

1 Combine 1 cup spinach, the shallots, jelly, vinegar, tarragon and salt in food processor or blender. Process until smooth. Add remaining 5 cups spinach, 1 cup at a time, processing after each addition until dressing is smooth.

2 Arrange greens and tomato slices on serving dishes. Spoon 2 tablespoons dressing over each serving. Refrigerate remaining dressing up to 1 week in airtight container.

Nutrition Facts	Amount/serving	%DV*	Amount/serving	%DV*
Serving Size 2 tablespoons (40g) Servings per Recipe 12 Calories 25 Calories from Fat 1	Total Fat <1g	0%	Total Carbohydrate 6g	2%
	Saturated Fat <1g	0%	Dietary Fiber 1g	4%
	Cholesterol 0mg	0%	Sugars 5g	
	Sodium 47mg	2%	Protein 1g	

Vitamin A 45% • Vitamin C 15% • Calcium 2% • Iron 4%

*Percent Daily Values (DV) are based on a 2000 calorie diet.

Menu Planning Guide
One serving of this recipe provides:
½ Vegetable

Diet Exchanges:
½ vegetable

MEATS

BRANDY PEPPER STEAKS

4 beef eye round steaks (4 oz. each), ¾ inch thick
1 to 3 teaspoons coarsely ground pepper
½ cup ready-to-serve beef broth
2 teaspoons cornstarch
4 oz. fresh mushrooms, sliced (1½ cups)
¼ cup sliced green onions
1 tablespoon brandy
¼ teaspoon salt

4 servings

Serving suggestion: Serve with boiled new potatoes and steamed broccoli spears.

1 Sprinkle both sides of steaks evenly with pepper. Set aside. In 1-quart saucepan, combine broth and cornstarch. Stir until blended. Stir in mushrooms, onions, brandy and salt. Cook over medium heat for 3 to 4 minutes, or until mixture is thickened and translucent, stirring constantly. Cover to keep warm. Remove from heat. Set sauce aside.

2 Spray 10-inch nonstick skillet with nonstick vegetable cooking spray. Heat skillet over medium-high heat. Cook steaks for 4 to 5 minutes, or until desired doneness, turning over once. Spoon sauce over steaks.

Nutrition Facts	Amount/serving	%DV*	Amount/serving	%DV*
Serving Size 1 steak (158g)	Total Fat 6g	9%	Total Carbohydrate 3g	1%
Servings per Recipe 4	Saturated Fat 2g	11%	Dietary Fiber 1g	3%
Calories 185	Cholesterol 64mg	21%	Sugars 1g	
Calories from Fat 55	Sodium 286mg	12%	Protein 28g	

Vitamin A 0% • Vitamin C 4% • Calcium 2% • Iron 15%
*Percent Daily Values (DV) are based on a 2000 calorie diet.

Menu Planning Guide
One serving of this recipe provides:
1 Meat, Poultry & Fish
½ Vegetable

Diet Exchanges:
1 lean meat • ½ vegetable

SZECHUAN BARBECUE PORK & VEGETABLES

½ cup light barbecue sauce
2 to 3 tablespoons honey
2 tablespoons reduced-sodium soy sauce
¼ to ½ teaspoon crushed red pepper flakes

1 well-trimmed pork tenderloin (12 oz.),
     cut into ½-inch slices
1 pkg. (10 oz.) frozen whole baby carrots
4 oz. fresh snow pea pods (1½ cups)
4 servings

1 Combine barbecue sauce, honey, soy sauce and red pepper flakes in 2-cup measure. Set aside. Spray 12-inch nonstick skillet or wok skillet with nonstick vegetable cooking spray. Heat skillet over medium heat. Add pork slices. Cook for 4 to 6 minutes, or just until no longer pink, stirring occasionally.

2 Add sauce mixture and carrots. Cook for 10 minutes. Add pea pods. Cook for 5 to 8 minutes, or until pea pods are bright green and mixture is hot, stirring occasionally. Serve over hot cooked rice, if desired.

Nutrition Facts	Amount/serving	%DV*	Amount/serving	%DV*	Menu Planning Guide
Serving Size 8 oz. (214g)	Total Fat 3g	5%	Total Carbohydrate 24g	8%	One serving of this recipe provides:
Servings per Recipe 4	Saturated Fat 1g	6%	Dietary Fiber 3g	13%	1 Meat, Poultry & Fish 1 Vegetable
Calories 214	Cholesterol 53mg	18%	Sugars 13g		
Calories from Fat 30	Sodium 613mg	26%	Protein 21g		

Vitamin A 130% • Vitamin C 35% • Calcium 4% • Iron 15%
*Percent Daily Values (DV) are based on a 2000 calorie diet.

Diet Exchanges:
2 lean meat • 1 starch • 1 vegetable

APPLE-SAGE STUFFED PORK LOIN ROAST

¼ cup apple jelly

1 tablespoon packed brown sugar

1½ teaspoons Dijon mustard

1 medium red cooking apple, cored and chopped (1 cup)

1 stalk celery, chopped (½ cup)

1 small onion, chopped (½ cup)

2 tablespoons vegetable oil

½ cup unseasoned dry bread crumbs

¼ cup snipped fresh parsley

2 tablespoons snipped fresh sage leaves

3-lb. well-trimmed boneless pork double loin roast

12 servings

1 Combine jelly, sugar and mustard in 1-quart saucepan. Cook over medium-low heat for 3½ to 5 minutes, or until jelly is melted, stirring constantly. Remove from heat. Set glaze aside.

2 Combine apple, celery, onion and oil in 2-quart saucepan. Cook over medium heat for 4 to 8 minutes, or until apple is tender, stirring frequently. Remove from heat. Add bread crumbs, parsley and sage. Mix well.

3 Heat oven to 325°F. Untie pork roast. Separate the 2 pieces of loin. Spoon and pack apple mixture on top of 1 piece. Place remaining piece over stuffing. Tie at 1½-inch intervals to secure.

4 Place roast on rack in broiler pan. Roast for 1 hour 40 minutes to 1 hour 50 minutes, or until internal temperature registers 155°F and juices run clear, basting with glaze during last 15 minutes. Let stand, tented with foil, for 10 minutes. (Internal temperature will rise 5°F during standing.)

Microwave tip: In 1-cup measure, combine jelly, sugar and mustard. Microwave at High for 1 to 2½ minutes, or until jelly is melted, stirring once. Continue as directed.

Nutrition Facts

Serving Size
 1/12 roast (106g)
Servings
 per Recipe 12
Calories 209
 Calories
 from Fat 83

Amount/serving	%DV*	Amount/serving	%DV*
Total Fat 9g	14%	Total Carbohydrate 11g	4%
Saturated Fat 3g	14%	Dietary Fiber <1g	3%
Cholesterol 55mg	18%	Sugars 7g	
Sodium 91mg	4%	Protein 20g	

Vitamin A 2% • Vitamin C 6% • Calcium 4% • Iron 8%

*Percent Daily Values (DV) are based on a 2000 calorie diet.

Menu Planning Guide

One serving of this recipe provides:
1 Meat, Poultry & Fish

Diet Exchanges:

2½ lean meat • ½ starch

VEAL SCALLOPS WITH MANDARIN ORANGE SAUCE

1 tablespoon cornstarch
1 can (11 oz.) mandarin orange segments,
　　drained (reserve juice)
2 tablespoons orange juice
1 tablespoon sliced green onion
1 tablespoon finely chopped red pepper
2 tablespoons all-purpose flour
1/2 teaspoon pepper
8 veal scallops (2 oz. each), 1/4 inch thick

4 servings

1 Place cornstarch in 1-quart saucepan. Blend in reserved juice and orange juice. Stir in onion and red pepper. Cook over medium-low heat for 4 to 6 minutes, or until sauce is thickened and translucent, stirring constantly. Stir in orange segments. Cover to keep warm. Set aside.

2 Combine flour and pepper in shallow dish. Dredge veal scallops in flour mixture, turning to coat both sides. Spray 10-inch nonstick skillet with nonstick vegetable cooking spray. Heat skillet over medium heat. Cook 4 scallops for 5 to 6 minutes, or until golden brown on both sides, turning over once. Place browned scallops on serving platter. Cover to keep warm. Clean skillet. Repeat procedure with remaining 4 scallops. Serve scallops with sauce.

Microwave tip: Place cornstarch in 2-cup measure. Blend in reserved juice and orange juice. Stir in onion and red pepper. Microwave at High for 2 to 3 minutes, or until sauce is thickened and translucent, stirring every minute. Continue as directed.

Nutrition Facts

Serving Size
　2 scallops (174g)
Servings
　per Recipe 4
Calories 230
　Calories
　from Fat 68

Amount/serving	%DV*	Amount/serving	%DV*
Total Fat 8g	11%	Total Carbohydrate 12g	4%
Saturated Fat 2g	10%	Dietary Fiber <1g	3%
Cholesterol 101mg	34%	Sugars 8g	
Sodium 73mg	3%	Protein 28g	

Vitamin A 8% • Vitamin C 60% • Calcium 4% • Iron 8%
*Percent Daily Values (DV) are based on a 2000 calorie diet.

Menu Planning Guide

One serving of this recipe provides:
1 Meat, Poultry & Fish
1 Fruit

Diet Exchanges:
3 lean meat • 1 fruit

SOUTHWESTERN-STYLE POT ROAST

Sauce:

- 1   can (8 oz.) tomato sauce
- 1/4   cup red wine vinegar
- 2   tablespoons tomato paste
- 2   teaspoons sugar
- 2   teaspoons dried oregano leaves
- 1   teaspoon ground cumin
- 1/2   teaspoon ground cinnamon
- 1/2   teaspoon freshly ground pepper
- 1/4   teaspoon salt

- 3-lb. well-trimmed bone-in beef chuck arm pot roast, 1½ inches thick
- 3   jalapeño peppers, seeded and cut into thin strips

- 1   medium onion, cut into 8 wedges
- 1   green pepper, cut into ½-inch strips
- 1/2   red pepper, cut into ½-inch strips
- 1/2   yellow pepper, cut into ½-inch strips

8 servings

Serving suggestion: Serve with baked potato, oven fries or hot cooked rice.

1 Combine all sauce ingredients in 2-cup measure. Set aside. Heat 12-inch skillet or 6-quart Dutch oven over medium heat. Add roast. Cook for 1½ to 2½ minutes, or until brown on both sides, turning over once. Drain.

2 Pour sauce over meat. Sprinkle jalapeño strips over sauce. Arrange onion around meat. Bring sauce to boil over medium-high heat. Cover. Reduce heat to low. Simmer roast for 2 hours, or until meat is tender.

3 Add green, red and yellow pepper strips. Re-cover. Simmer for 15 to 20 minutes, or until pepper strips are tender-crisp.

4 Carve meat across grain into thin slices. Top with sauce and peppers. Serve extra sauce separately.

Nutrition Facts	Amount/serving	%DV*	Amount/serving	%DV*
Serving Size 1/8 roast (154g)	Total Fat 6g	9%	Total Carbohydrate 7g	2%
Servings per Recipe 8	Saturated Fat 2g	11%	Dietary Fiber 1g	6%
Calories 180	Cholesterol 70mg	23%	Sugars 4g	
Calories from Fat 54	Sodium 377mg	16%	Protein 24g	
	Vitamin A 8% • Vitamin C 80% • Calcium 2% • Iron 20%			
	*Percent Daily Values (DV) are based on a 2000 calorie diet.			

Menu Planning Guide

One serving of this recipe provides:
1. Meat, Poultry & Fish
1. Vegetable

Diet Exchanges:

2½ lean meat • 1 vegetable

RAGOUT* OF LAMB

1-lb. well-trimmed boneless lamb leg roast,
    cut into ¾-inch pieces
1 can (14½ oz.) diced tomatoes
2 medium carrots, cut into 1½ x ¼-inch strips
    (1½ cups)
2 teaspoons chili powder
¼ to ½ teaspoon ground cinnamon
½ teaspoon sugar
¼ teaspoon salt
1 cup green pepper chunks (½-inch chunks)

4 servings

*Serving suggestion: Serve over hot cooked couscous
or rice.*

** Ragout is a thick, well-seasoned stew of meat,
poultry or fish, made with or without vegetables.
It is from a French word meaning "to stimulate
the appetite."*

1 Spray 12-inch nonstick skillet with nonstick vegetable cooking spray. Add lamb. Cook over medium heat for 4 to 6 minutes, or just until meat is only slightly pink, stirring occasionally. Drain.

2 Stir in remaining ingredients, except pepper chunks. Cover. Cook over medium heat for 10 minutes, stirring occasionally. Stir in pepper chunks. Re-cover. Cook over medium heat for 7 to 9 minutes, or until vegetables are tender, stirring occasionally.

Microwave tip: Place lamb in 3-quart casserole. Cover. Microwave at High for 6 to 8 minutes, or just until meat is only slightly pink, stirring once or twice. Drain. Stir in remaining ingredients, except pepper chunks. Re-cover. Microwave at High for 5 minutes. Stir in pepper chunks. Re-cover. Microwave at High for 8 to 11 minutes, or until vegetables are tender, stirring twice.

Nutrition Facts	Amount/serving	%DV*	Amount/serving	%DV*
Serving Size 1 cup (238g)	Total Fat 6g	10%	Total Carbohydrate 11g	4%
Servings per Recipe 4	Saturated Fat 2g	10%	Dietary Fiber 3g	12%
Calories 188	Cholesterol 64mg	21%	Sugars 6g	
Calories from Fat 56	Sodium 376mg	16%	Protein 22g	

Vitamin A 230% • Vitamin C 70% • Calcium 6% • Iron 15%
*Percent Daily Values (DV) are based on a 2000 calorie diet.

Menu Planning Guide
One serving of this recipe provides:
1 Meat, Poultry & Fish
2 Vegetable

Diet Exchanges:
2½ lean meat • 2 vegetable

SPICY BEEF WITH PEPPERS & ORANGES

1-lb. well-trimmed beef top sirloin steak, 1 inch
    thick, cut into 2 x ⅛-inch strips
1 medium seedless orange
1 tablespoon reduced-sodium soy sauce
½ teaspoon ground ginger
½ teaspoon cayenne
⅛ teaspoon garlic powder

1½ teaspoons cornstarch
½ cup water
2 cups red or green pepper chunks
    (¾-inch chunks)

4 servings

Serving suggestion: Serve over hot cooked ramen
noodles, fine egg noodles or rice.

1 Place beef strips in medium mixing bowl. Set aside. Grate 1½ teaspoons peel from orange. Set aside. Remove and discard remaining peel. Cut orange into ¼-inch slices. Cut each slice in half. Set aside. Sprinkle meat with 1 teaspoon reserved peel, the soy sauce, ginger, cayenne and garlic powder. Toss to coat.

2 Spray 12-inch nonstick skillet with nonstick vegetable cooking spray. Heat skillet over medium heat. Add meat mixture. Cook for 2 to 3 minutes, or until meat is only slightly pink, stirring frequently. Using slotted spoon, remove meat from skillet. Set aside.

3 Wipe skillet with paper towel. In same skillet, combine cornstarch and remaining ½ teaspoon peel. Blend in water. Add pepper chunks. Cook over medium heat for 3 to 5 minutes, or until mixture is thickened and translucent and peppers are tender-crisp, stirring frequently. Stir in meat and orange pieces. Cook 1½ to 2 minutes, or until hot, stirring occasionally.

Nutrition Facts	Amount/serving	%DV*	Amount/serving	%DV*
Serving Size approximately 1 cup (226g) Servings per Recipe 4 Calories 216 Calories from Fat 60	Total Fat 7g	10%	Total Carbohydrate 10g	3%
	Saturated Fat 3g	13%	Dietary Fiber 2g	8%
	Cholesterol 80mg	27%	Sugars 5g	
	Sodium 211mg	9%	Protein 28g	

Vitamin A 70% • Vitamin C 210% • Calcium 4% • Iron 20%
*Percent Daily Values (DV) are based on a 2000 calorie diet.

Menu Planning Guide
One serving of this recipe provides:
1 Meat, Poultry & Fish
1 Vegetable

Diet Exchanges:
3 lean meat • 1 vegetable

BEEF EYE ROUND STEAKS WITH VEGETABLES

12 oz. new potatoes, sliced (2 cups), rinsed and
    drained
 1 pkg. (10 oz.) frozen peas and carrots
 1 cup water
 1 tablespoon margarine
 1 tablespoon all-purpose flour
½ teaspoon salt
½ teaspoon dried marjoram
¼ teaspoon pepper
¾ cup skim milk
 4 beef eye round steaks (4 oz. each), ¾ inch thick

4 servings

1 Combine potatoes, peas, carrots and water in 3-quart saucepan. Cover. Cook over medium-high heat for 14 to 18 minutes, or until vegetables are tender, stirring occasionally. Drain. Return vegetables to saucepan. Cover to keep warm. Set aside.

2 Melt margarine over medium-low heat in 1-quart saucepan. Stir in flour, salt, marjoram and pepper. Gradually blend in milk. Cook for 7 to 12 minutes, or until mixture thickens and bubbles, stirring frequently. Add sauce to vegetable mixture. Toss to combine. Re-cover. Set aside.

3 Spray rack in broiler pan with nonstick vegetable cooking spray. Arrange steaks on rack. Place under broiler with surface of meat 3 to 5 inches from heat. Broil for 13 to 15 minutes, or until desired doneness, turning steaks over once. Serve steaks with vegetable mixture.

Microwave tip: In 4-cup measure, microwave margarine at High for 45 seconds to 1 minute, or until melted. Stir in flour, salt, marjoram and pepper. Gradually blend in milk. Microwave at High for 2½ to 3½ minutes, or until mixture thickens and bubbles, stirring every minute. Continue as directed.

Nutrition Facts	Amount/serving	%DV*	Amount/serving	%DV*
Serving Size 1 steak (294g)	Total Fat 8g	12%	Total Carbohydrate 27g	9%
Servings per Recipe 4	Saturated Fat 2g	12%	Dietary Fiber 4g	16%
Calories 303	Cholesterol 63mg	21%	Sugars 6g	
Calories from Fat 68	Sodium 431mg	18%	Protein 32g	

Vitamin A 110% • Vitamin C 30% • Calcium 8% • Iron 15%
*Percent Daily Values (DV) are based on a 2000 calorie diet.

Menu Planning Guide
One serving of this recipe provides:
1 Meat, Poultry & Fish
2 Vegetable

Diet Exchanges:
3 lean meat • 1½ starch • ½ vegetable

PLUM-SAUCED PORK MEDALLIONS

¼ cup chopped onion

½ teaspoon vegetable oil

½ cup red plum jam

1 tablespoon red wine vinegar

1 teaspoon reduced-sodium soy sauce

¼ teaspoon ground ginger

2 small plums, each cut into 8 wedges

1 well-trimmed pork tenderloin (approx. 1 lb.), cut crosswise into 8 pieces

Cayenne

4 servings

Serving suggestion: Serve with hot cooked wide egg noodles tossed with poppy seed.

1 Spray 8-inch nonstick skillet with nonstick vegetable cooking spray. Add onion and oil. Cook over medium heat for 4 to 7 minutes, or until onion is tender, stirring occasionally. Reduce heat to low. Stir in jam, vinegar, soy sauce and ginger. Cook for 1 to 2 minutes, or until jam is melted, stirring occasionally. Stir in plums. Set sauce aside.

2 Pound pork pieces lightly to 1-inch thickness. Sprinkle both sides of each piece lightly with cayenne. Spray 10-inch nonstick skillet with nonstick vegetable cooking spray. Heat skillet over medium-high heat. Add pork. Cook for 6 to 8 minutes, or just until meat is no longer pink, turning over once. Serve topped with plum sauce.

Microwave tip: Omit oil. Place onion in 2-cup measure. Cover with plastic wrap. Microwave at High for 2 to 3 minutes, or until tender, stirring once. Stir in jam, vinegar, soy sauce and ginger. Microwave at High, uncovered, for 1½ to 2 minutes, or until jam is melted, stirring once. Stir in plums. Set sauce aside. Continue as directed.

Nutrition Facts	Amount/serving	%DV*	Amount/serving	%DV*
Serving Size 2 medallions w/sauce (156g)	Total Fat 5g	8%	Total Carbohydrate 31g	10%
Servings per Recipe 4	Saturated Fat 2g	8%	Dietary Fiber 1g	4%
	Cholesterol 70mg	23%	Sugars 30g	
Calories 272	Sodium 108mg	5%	Protein 26g	
Calories from Fat 45	Vitamin A 2% • Vitamin C 4% • Calcium 2% • Iron 10%			
	*Percent Daily Values (DV) are based on a 2000 calorie diet.			

Menu Planning Guide

One serving of this recipe provides:

1 Meat, Poultry & Fish

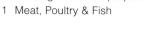

Diet Exchanges:

3 lean meat • 2 fruit

BROILED FRUITED PORK CHOPS

6 *well-trimmed boneless pork loin chops*
   (4 oz. each), ½ inch thick
1 *can (8 oz.) pineapple slices in juice, drained*
   (reserve ¼ cup juice)
1 *can (16 oz.) apricot halves in juice, drained*

¼ *cup apricot preserves*
2 *teaspoons Dijon mustard*
2 *teaspoons cider vinegar*

6 servings

1 Arrange pork chops on rack in broiler pan. Cut pineapple slices in half. Arrange pineapple and apricots evenly around chops. Set aside. In 1-quart saucepan, combine preserves, mustard and vinegar. Cook over low heat for 5 to 8 minutes, or until preserves are melted, stirring occasionally.

2 Brush chops with half of preserves mixture. Brush pineapple and apricots with half of reserved pineapple juice. Place chops under broiler with surface of meat 3 to 4 inches from heat. Broil for 10 to 12 minutes, or until desired doneness, turning chops over and basting chops with remaining preserves mixture and fruit with remaining juice once.

Microwave tip: In 2-cup measure, combine preserves, mustard and vinegar. Microwave at High for 2 to 3 minutes, or until preserves are melted, stirring once. Continue as directed.

Nutrition Facts	Amount/serving	%DV*	Amount/serving	%DV*
Serving Size 1 chop (207g)	Total Fat 7g	11%	Total Carbohydrate 22g	7%
Servings per Recipe 6	Saturated Fat 2g	12%	Dietary Fiber 2g	8%
Calories 252	Cholesterol 67mg	22%	Sugars 19g	
Calories from Fat 64	Sodium 77mg	3%	Protein 26g	

Vitamin A 35% • Vitamin C 25% • Calcium 4% • Iron 8%
*Percent Daily Values (DV) are based on a 2000 calorie diet.

Menu Planning Guide
One serving of this recipe provides:
1 Meat, Poultry & Fish
1 Fruit

Diet Exchanges:
3 lean meat • 1½ fruit

POULTRY

ORANGE CHICKEN VÉRONIQUE*

1 tablespoon vegetable oil
3 bone-in whole chicken breasts (10 to 12 oz. each),
   split in half, skin removed
½ cup orange juice
½ cup dry white wine
1 teaspoon sugar
¼ teaspoon salt
¼ teaspoon dried marjoram leaves
⅛ teaspoon white pepper
1 tablespoon cornstarch mixed with
   1 tablespoon water

½ cup halved seedless green grapes
½ cup halved seedless red grapes
1 teaspoon grated orange peel

6 servings

*Véronique is a term used to describe dishes
garnished with grapes, usually seedless green grapes.*

1 Place oil in 12-inch nonstick skillet. Heat over medium-high heat. Add chicken. Cook for 4 to 6 minutes, or just until browned on both sides. Drain excess oil from skillet.

2 Add juice, wine, sugar, salt, marjoram and pepper to skillet. Cover. Reduce heat to low. Let simmer for 12 to 15 minutes, or until meat near bone is no longer pink and juices run clear.

3 Remove chicken from skillet and place on serving platter. Cover to keep warm. Set aside. Using whisk, stir cornstarch mixture into skillet. Add grapes and peel. Cook for 1½ to 2½ minutes, or until sauce is thickened and translucent, stirring constantly. Spoon over chicken.

Nutrition Facts	Amount/serving	%DV*	Amount/serving	%DV*
Serving Size 1 breast half (136g)	Total Fat 5g	7%	Total Carbohydrate 9g	3%
	Saturated Fat 1g	5%	Dietary Fiber <1g	1%
Servings per Recipe 6	Cholesterol 55mg	18%	Sugars 8g	
Calories 164 Calories from Fat 41	Sodium 135mg	6%	Protein 21g	

Vitamin A 0% • Vitamin C 20% • Calcium 2% • Iron 4%
*Percent Daily Values (DV) are based on a 2000 calorie diet.

Menu Planning Guide
One serving of this recipe provides:
  1 Meat, Poultry & Fish
  ½ Fruit

Diet Exchanges:
3 lean meat • ½ fruit

TURKEY MARSALA

½ cup ready-to-serve chicken broth

3 tablespoons Marsala wine

1 tablespoon cornstarch

8 oz. fresh mushrooms, sliced (3 cups)

1 medium carrot, cut into 2 x ¼-inch
  strips (½ cup)

1 tablespoon snipped fresh parsley

2 turkey tenderloins (8 to 10 oz. each)

¼ teaspoon freshly ground pepper

6 servings

*Serving suggestion: Serve with Brown Rice with
Toasted Pine Nuts (see page 182).*

1 Combine broth, wine and cornstarch in 1-cup
measure. Set aside. Heat 12-inch nonstick
skillet with lid over medium heat. Add mushrooms, carrot strips, parsley and broth mixture.
Cook for 4 to 6 minutes, or until mushrooms are
tender and sauce is thickened and translucent,
stirring frequently.

2 Sprinkle tenderloins evenly with pepper. Add
tenderloins to skillet, turning to coat. Cover.
Reduce heat to low. Cook for 20 to 25 minutes,
or until meat is firm and no longer pink.

Nutrition Facts	Amount/serving	%DV*	Amount/serving	%DV*
Serving Size 3-4 oz. (131g)	Total Fat 3g	5%	Total Carbohydrate 4g	1%
Servings per Recipe 6	Saturated Fat 1g	5%	Dietary Fiber 1g	4%
Calories 122	Cholesterol 44mg	15%	Sugars 1g	
Calories from Fat 27	Sodium 111mg	5%	Protein 18g	

Vitamin A 35% • Vitamin C 6% • Calcium 2% • Iron 10%
*Percent Daily Values (DV) are based on a 2000 calorie diet.

Menu Planning Guide

One serving of this recipe provides:

1 Meat, Poultry & Fish
½ Vegetable

Diet Exchanges:

2 lean meat • ½ vegetable

CHICKEN GUMBO

1/4 cup all-purpose flour
1 can (14 1/2 oz.) ready-to-serve chicken broth, defatted*, divided
1 medium red pepper, chopped (1 cup)
3/4 cup sliced celery
7 green onions, white portions sliced, green tops cut into 3-inch lengths and reserved
2 cloves garlic, minced
1 can (15 oz.) black-eyed peas, rinsed and drained
2 medium tomatoes, chopped (2 cups)
1 can (4 oz.) diced green chilies
1/4 cup snipped fresh parsley
1 teaspoon dried thyme leaves

1/2 teaspoon pepper
1/8 teaspoon red pepper sauce
8 bone-in chicken thighs (5 oz. each), skin removed
1/2 teaspoon Cajun seasoning
1 pkg. (10 oz.) frozen cut okra, defrosted

8 servings

Defat broth by chilling 4 hours; skim and discard solidified fat from surface.

1 Heat oven to 400°F. Sprinkle flour evenly into 8-inch square baking pan. Bake for 10 to 15 minutes, or until deep golden brown, stirring every 5 minutes. Set aside.

2 Combine 1/2 cup broth, the red pepper, celery, white portions of onions and the garlic in 4-quart saucepan. Cook over medium-high heat for 4 to 5 minutes, or until vegetables are tender-crisp, stirring occasionally. Stir in flour. Blend in remaining broth, the peas, tomatoes, chilies, parsley, thyme, pepper and red pepper sauce.

3 Rub chicken with Cajun seasoning. Add to gumbo. Bring gumbo to boil over high heat. Cover. Reduce heat to low. Simmer for 25 to 35 minutes, or until meat near bone on chicken is no longer pink and juices run clear. (If desired, remove chicken and cut meat from bones. Discard bones. Return meat to gumbo.)

4 Stir in reserved onion tops and the okra. Cook for 4 to 5 minutes, or until onion tops are wilted and mixture thickens slightly. Serve over hot cooked rice and sprinkle with filé powder, if desired. (Filé powder is a seasoning made from dried sassafras leaves, used to flavor and thicken Creole dishes.)

Nutrition Facts	Amount/serving	%DV*	Amount/serving	%DV*
Serving Size approximately 1 cup (282g)	Total Fat 7g	10%	Total Carbohydrate 20g	7%
Servings per Recipe 8	Saturated Fat 2g	9%	Dietary Fiber 6g	23%
Calories 233	Cholesterol 56mg	19%	Sugars 4g	
Calories from Fat 59	Sodium 320mg	13%	Protein 23g	

Vitamin A 15% • Vitamin C 70% • Calcium 8% • Iron 20%
*Percent Daily Values (DV) are based on a 2000 calorie diet.

Menu Planning Guide
One serving of this recipe provides:
1 Meat, Poultry & Fish
1 Vegetable

Diet Exchanges:
2 lean meat • 1 starch • 1 vegetable

LIME & CUMIN CORNISH GAME HENS

1/4 cup dark corn syrup
1/2 to 1 teaspoon grated lime peel
 2 tablespoons lime juice
 1 teaspoon ground cumin, divided
 4 Cornish game hens (24 oz. each)
1/2 teaspoon dried oregano leaves

1/4 teaspoon salt
1/8 teaspoon pepper

8 servings

1 Combine syrup, peel, juice and 1/2 teaspoon cumin in small bowl. Set aside.

2 Secure hens' legs together with string. Place hens in large plastic food-storage bag. Pour syrup mixture over hens. Secure bag and place in dish. Refrigerate at least 2 hours, turning bag over once.

3 Heat oven to 350°F. Remove hens from marinade and arrange breast-side-up on rack in shallow roasting pan. Discard marinade. In small bowl, combine remaining 1/2 teaspoon cumin and remaining ingredients. Rub hens with mixture.

4 Bake for 45 minutes to 1 hour, or until internal temperature in thickest portions of thighs registers 185°F. Cut hens in half lengthwise before serving. Before eating, remove and discard skin.

Nutrition Facts	Amount/serving	%DV*	Amount/serving	%DV*
Serving Size 1/2 hen (117g)	Total Fat 8g	12%	Total Carbohydrate <1g	0%
Servings per Recipe 8	Saturated Fat 2g	11%	Dietary Fiber <1g	0%
Calories 195	Cholesterol 87mg	29%	Sugars <1g	
Calories from Fat 69	Sodium 154mg	6%	Protein 29g	

Vitamin A 2% • Vitamin C 0% • Calcium 2% • Iron 8%
*Percent Daily Values (DV) are based on a 2000 calorie diet.

Menu Planning Guide
One serving of this recipe provides:
1 1/2 Meat, Poultry & Fish

Diet Exchanges:
4 lean meat

SPRING LEMON CHICKEN

3 bone-in whole chicken breasts
   (10 to 12 oz. each), split in half, skin removed
1/8 teaspoon white pepper
1 teaspoon olive oil
1 tablespoon grated lemon peel
2 tablespoons fresh lemon juice
1 tablespoon honey

6 servings

*Serving suggestion: Serve with boiled new potatoes
and chives, and steamed asparagus spears.*

1 Sprinkle chicken evenly with pepper. In 12-inch nonstick skillet, heat oil over medium-high heat. Add chicken. Cook for 4 to 6 minutes, or just until brown on both sides. Reduce heat to low.

2 Combine peel, juice and honey in small bowl. Brush honey mixture on both sides of chicken pieces. Cover. Cook for 14 to 17 minutes, or until meat near bone is no longer pink and juices run clear.

Nutrition Facts	Amount/serving	%DV*	Amount/serving	%DV*
Serving Size 1/2 breast (91g)	Total Fat 4g	6%	Total Carbohydrate 4g	1%
Servings per Recipe 6	Saturated Fat <1g	5%	Dietary Fiber <1g	0%
Calories 152	Cholesterol 69mg	23%	Sugars 3g	
Calories from Fat 33	Sodium 60mg	3%	Protein 25g	
	Vitamin A 0% • Vitamin C 6% • Calcium 2% • Iron 4%			
	*Percent Daily Values (DV) are based on a 2000 calorie diet.			

Menu Planning Guide
One serving of this recipe provides:
1 Meat, Poultry & Fish

Diet Exchanges:
3 lean meat

TURKEY TETRAZZINI

8 oz. uncooked spaghetti,
   broken into 2-inch lengths
1/4 cup margarine, divided
1 cup sliced fresh mushrooms
1 stalk celery, sliced (1/2 cup)
1 clove garlic, minced
3 tablespoons all-purpose flour
2 1/2 cups skim milk
1/4 teaspoon salt

1/4 to 1/2 teaspoon pepper
1 1/2 cups cubed fully cooked turkey breast
   or lean ham (3/4-inch cubes)
1/3 cup shredded low-fat Swiss cheese
1 jar (2 oz.) sliced pimiento, drained

8 servings

1 Prepare spaghetti as directed on package. Rinse and drain. Set aside.

2 Heat oven to 350°F. In 2-quart saucepan, combine 1 tablespoon margarine, the mushrooms, celery and garlic. Cook over medium heat for 5 to 7 minutes, or until celery is tender-crisp, stirring occasionally. Stir in remaining 3 tablespoons margarine until melted. Stir in flour. Cook for 30 seconds to 1 minute, or until mixture bubbles.

3 Blend in milk, salt and pepper. Cook over medium heat for 10 minutes, stirring frequently. Reduce heat to low and cook for 2 to 5 minutes longer, or until sauce thickens and bubbles, stirring occasionally. In 2-quart casserole, combine sauce, spaghetti and remaining ingredients. Bake for 30 to 35 minutes, or until hot.

Nutrition Facts	Amount/serving	%DV*	Amount/serving	%DV*	Menu Planning Guide
Serving Size approximately 1 cup (211g)	Total Fat 7g	11%	Total Carbohydrate 27g	9%	One serving of this recipe provides:
Servings per Recipe 8	Saturated Fat 2g	8%	Dietary Fiber 2g	7%	1/2 Milk, Yogurt & Cheese
	Cholesterol 21mg	7%	Sugars 5g		1/2 Meat, Poultry & Fish
Calories 241	Sodium 212mg	9%	Protein 16g		1 Bread, Cereal, Rice & Pasta
Calories from Fat 67	Vitamin A 10% • Vitamin C 10% • Calcium 15% • Iron 10%				
	*Percent Daily Values (DV) are based on a 2000 calorie diet.				

Diet Exchanges:
1 lean meat • 1/2 skim milk • 1 starch • 1 fat

CHICKEN MARENGO

3-lb. whole broiler-fryer chicken, cut into 8
   pieces, skin removed

1 medium onion, thinly sliced and separated
   into rings

2 medium carrots, cut into 1½ x ¼-inch strips
   (1 cup)

¼ cup water

1 teaspoon olive oil

1 can (14½ oz.) whole tomatoes, undrained and
   cut up

3 tablespoons tomato paste

1 tablespoon brandy

½ teaspoon sugar

½ teaspoon dried marjoram leaves

¼ teaspoon salt

¼ teaspoon garlic powder

⅛ teaspoon pepper

2 cups hot cooked white rice

4 servings

1 Spray 12-inch nonstick skillet with nonstick vegetable cooking spray. Heat skillet over medium-high heat. Add chicken. Cook for 4 to 6 minutes, or just until brown on both sides. Remove chicken from skillet. Cover to keep warm. Set aside.

2 Reduce heat to medium. In same skillet, combine onion, carrot, water and oil. Cook for 5 to 8 minutes, or until carrots are tender-crisp, stirring frequently. Stir in remaining ingredients, except rice. Cook for 1 to 2 minutes, or until sauce is hot, stirring occasionally.

3 Arrange chicken over sauce in skillet. Spoon some of sauce over chicken. Cover. Cook for 12 to 15 minutes, or until meat near bone is no longer pink and juices run clear, turning chicken over once. To serve, arrange chicken over rice on serving platter and spoon sauce over chicken. Garnish with snipped fresh parsley, if desired.

Nutrition Facts	Amount/serving	%DV*	Amount/serving	%DV*	Menu Planning Guide
Serving Size 2 pieces chicken (373g)	Total Fat 10g	15%	Total Carbohydrate 40g	13%	One serving of this recipe provides:
Servings per Recipe 4	Saturated Fat 2g	12%	Dietary Fiber 3g	12%	1 Meat, Poultry & Fish
	Cholesterol 92mg	31%	Sugars 6g		2 Vegetable
Calories 389	Sodium 497mg	21%	Protein 35g		1 Bread, Cereal, Rice & Pasta
Calories from Fat 86	Vitamin A 80% • Vitamin C 35% • Calcium 6% • Iron 20%				
	*Percent Daily Values (DV) are based on a 2000 calorie diet.				

Diet Exchanges:
3½ lean meat • 2 starch • 2 vegetable

LEMON THYME CHICKEN WITH VEGETABLES

1½ teaspoons dried thyme leaves, divided

1 teaspoon grated lemon peel

½ teaspoon salt, divided

¼ teaspoon pepper, divided

2 bone-in whole chicken breasts
(10 to 12 oz. each), split in half, skin removed

⅓ cup plus ¼ cup water, divided

1 tablespoon fresh lemon juice

1 cup green pepper strips (2 x ¼-inch strips)

1 cup red pepper strips (2 x ¼-inch strips)

1 medium zucchini, cut into 2 x ¼-inch strips
(1 cup)

1 medium carrot, thinly sliced (½ cup)

4 servings

1 Combine ¾ teaspoon thyme, the peel, ¼ teaspoon salt and ⅛ teaspoon pepper in small bowl. Rub chicken with mixture. Spray 10-inch nonstick skillet with nonstick vegetable cooking spray. Heat skillet over medium-high heat. Add chicken. Cook for 4 to 6 minutes, or just until brown on both sides. Reduce heat to low. Add ⅓ cup water and the juice to skillet. Cover. Cook for 20 to 24 minutes, or until meat near bone is no longer pink and juices run clear.

2 Meanwhile, combine pepper strips, zucchini, carrot, remaining ¼ cup water, ¾ teaspoon thyme, ¼ teaspoon salt and ⅛ teaspoon pepper in 2-quart saucepan. Cover. Cook over high heat for 4 to 6 minutes, or until vegetables are tender-crisp. Drain. Serve vegetables with chicken.

Microwave tip: Omit ¼ cup water. In 2-quart casserole, combine pepper strips, zucchini, carrot, remaining ¾ teaspoon thyme, ¼ teaspoon salt and ⅛ teaspoon pepper. Cover. Microwave at High for 4 to 5 minutes, or until vegetables are tender-crisp, stirring twice. Serve vegetables with chicken.

Nutrition Facts	Amount/serving	%DV*	Amount/serving	%DV*
Serving Size ½ breast (209g)	Total Fat 3g	4%	Total Carbohydrate 8g	3%
Servings per Recipe 4	Saturated Fat <1g	4%	Dietary Fiber 2g	8%
Calories 144	Cholesterol 57mg	19%	Sugars 3g	
Calories from Fat 24	Sodium 330mg	14%	Protein 22g	

Vitamin A 120% • Vitamin C 140% • Calcium 4% • Iron 10%
*Percent Daily Values (DV) are based on a 2000 calorie diet.

Menu Planning Guide
One serving of this recipe provides:

1 Meat, Poultry & Fish
1½ Vegetable

Diet Exchanges:
2½ lean meat • 1½ vegetable

TURKEY-STUFFED CABBAGE ROLLS

12 cups water
 6 large green cabbage leaves
 1 lb. ground turkey (breast meat only; no skin),
    crumbled
 1 small onion, chopped (½ cup)
 2 cloves garlic, minced, divided
 1 cup cooked wild rice
1½ teaspoons dried oregano leaves, divided
 1 teaspoon pepper, divided

¼ teaspoon salt
 1 can (8 oz.) tomato sauce
¼ teaspoon dried basil leaves

6 servings

1 Heat oven to 375°F. In 4-quart saucepan, bring water to boil over high heat. Immerse cabbage leaves in water for 1 minute, or until color brightens. Immediately plunge leaves into ice water. Drain. Set aside.

2 Combine turkey, onion and 1 clove garlic in 10-inch skillet. Cook over medium heat for 6 to 8 minutes, or until meat is no longer pink and onion is tender-crisp, stirring frequently. Drain. Stir in rice, 1 teaspoon oregano, ½ teaspoon pepper and the salt.

3 Spoon ½ cup turkey mixture into center of each cabbage leaf. Roll up leaves, folding in sides. Place cabbage rolls, seam-side-down, in 8-inch square baking dish. Set aside.

4 Combine remaining clove garlic, ½ teaspoon oregano, ½ teaspoon pepper, the tomato sauce and basil in 1-cup measure. Pour sauce evenly over rolls. Cover with foil. Bake for 25 to 30 minutes, or until centers of rolls are hot and sauce is bubbly. Spoon sauce over rolls when serving.

Nutrition Facts	Amount/serving	%DV*	Amount/serving	%DV*	Menu Planning Guide
Serving Size 1 roll (156g)	Total Fat 1g	2%	Total Carbohydrate 12g	4%	One serving of this recipe provides:
Servings per Recipe 6	Saturated Fat <1g	1%	Dietary Fiber 2g	8%	1 Meat, Poultry & Fish 1 Vegetable
Calories 133	Cholesterol 50mg	17%	Sugars 3g		
Calories from Fat 9	Sodium 355mg	15%	Protein 20g		

Vitamin A 8% • Vitamin C 20% • Calcium 4% • Iron 10%
*Percent Daily Values (DV) are based on a 2000 calorie diet.

Diet Exchanges:
2 lean meat • ½ starch • 1 vegetable

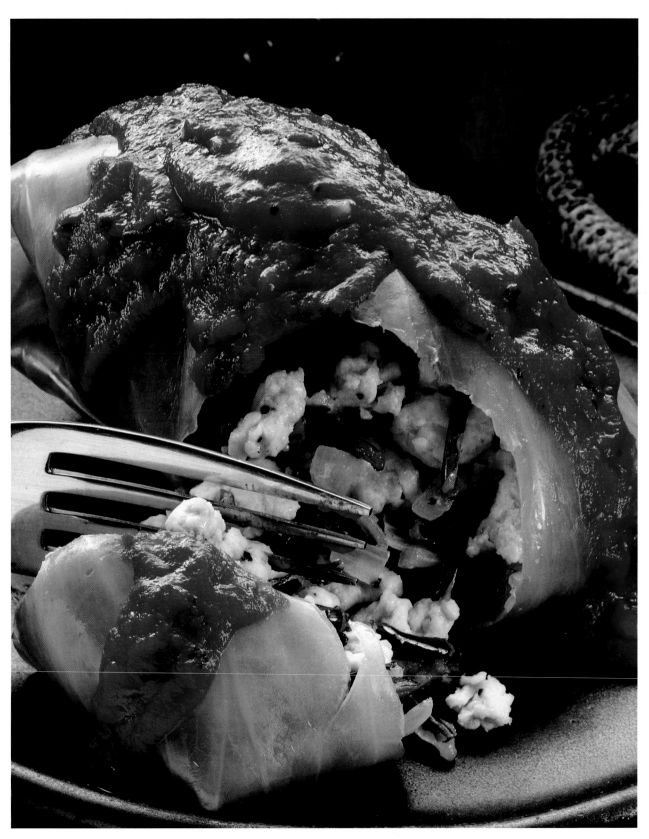

FISH & SEAFOOD

CHINESE-STYLE STEAMED TROUT

2   whole drawn stream trout (8 oz. each)
1   tablespoon grated fresh gingerroot
1   tablespoon minced garlic
2   teaspoons fermented Chinese black beans*,
     rinsed and drained
4   chopsticks or metal skewers
2   tablespoons reduced-sodium soy sauce
2   tablespoons dry white wine

2   green onions, cut diagonally into 2 x ⅛-inch
     strips
1   medium carrot, cut into 2 x ⅛-inch strips (½ cup)

2 servings

* Fermented Chinese black beans are small black soy
beans that have been preserved in salt. They are used
as a flavoring in fish or meat dishes.

1 Heat oven to 400°F. Score both sides of each fish in crisscross pattern, with cuts approximately ¼ inch deep and ½ inch apart. Set aside. In small mixing bowl, combine gingerroot, garlic and beans. Place 1 teaspoon gingerroot mixture in cavity of each fish.

2 Arrange chopsticks crosswise in 13 x 9-inch baking dish. Place fish on chopsticks. Spoon soy sauce over fish. Top evenly with remaining gingerroot mixture. Pour wine in bottom of dish.

3 Crisscross onion and carrot strips on each fish. Cover dish with foil. Bake for 12 to 14 minutes, or until fish begins to flake when fork is inserted at backbone in thickest part of fish.

Nutrition Facts	Amount/serving	%DV*	Amount/serving	%DV*	Menu Planning Guide
Serving Size 1 trout (162g)	Total Fat 4g	6%	Total Carbohydrate 11g	4%	One serving of this recipe provides:
Servings per Recipe 2	Saturated Fat 1g	5%	Dietary Fiber 3g	11%	1 Meat, Poultry & Fish 1 Vegetable
Calories 150	Cholesterol 43mg	14%	Sugars 3g		
Calories from Fat 35	Sodium 535mg	22%	Protein 17g		
	Vitamin A 100% • Vitamin C 15% • Calcium 8% • Iron 8%				
	*Percent Daily Values (DV) are based on a 2000 calorie diet.				**Diet Exchanges:** 2 lean meat • 1 starch

134

VEGETABLE-SHRIMP STIR-FRY

1 tablespoon vegetable oil
1 pkg. (9 oz.) frozen broccoli cuts
2 medium carrots, cut into 2 x ¼-inch
   strips (1 cup)
2 cloves garlic, minced
1 pkg. (10 oz.) frozen cooked shrimp, defrosted
   and drained

3 oz. fresh snow pea pods (1 cup)
2 tablespoons reduced-sodium soy sauce
2 tablespoons water
1 tablespoon cornstarch
½ teaspoon grated fresh gingerroot

4 servings

1 Heat wok or wok skillet over medium-high heat. Add oil, broccoli, carrot strips and garlic. Cook for 5 to 7 minutes, or until broccoli is defrosted, stirring frequently. Add shrimp and pea pods. Cook for 2 to 4 minutes, or until pea pods are bright green and mixture is hot, stirring frequently.

2 Combine remaining ingredients in 1-cup measure. Add to wok. Cook for 30 to 45 seconds, or until sauce is thickened and translucent, stirring constantly. Serve over hot cooked rice, if desired.

Nutrition Facts	Amount/serving	%DV*	Amount/serving	%DV*	Menu Planning Guide
Serving Size 8 oz. (237g)	Total Fat 5g	7%	Total Carbohydrate 13g	4%	One serving of this recipe provides:
Servings per Recipe 4	Saturated Fat 1g	4%	Dietary Fiber 3g	17%	1 Meat, Poultry & Fish 1 Vegetable
Calories 166	Cholesterol 138mg	46%	Sugars 6g		
Calories from Fat 40	Sodium 434mg	18%	Protein 19g		

Vitamin A 110% • Vitamin C 130% • Calcium 10% • Iron 20%
*Percent Daily Values (DV) are based on a 2000 calorie diet.

Diet Exchanges:
2 lean meat • ½ starch • 1 vegetable

ORANGE-SAUCED ROUGHY

½ cup fresh orange juice

⅓ cup ready-to-serve chicken broth
  or dry white wine

2 teaspoons cornstarch

1 teaspoon sugar

¼ teaspoon dried thyme leaves

1 lb. orange roughy fillets, about ½ inch thick,
  cut into serving-size pieces

1 teaspoon vegetable oil

4 servings

1 Combine juice, broth, cornstarch, sugar and thyme in 1-quart saucepan. Cook over medium heat for 3 to 5 minutes, or until sauce is thickened and translucent, stirring constantly. Remove from heat. Set aside.

2 Heat broiler. Spray large baking sheet with nonstick vegetable cooking spray. Arrange fillets on sheet. Brush fillets evenly with oil.

3 Place under broiler with surface of fillets 5 inches from heat. Broil for 9 to 13 minutes, or until fish is firm and opaque and just begins to flake. Arrange fish on serving platter. Top with sauce.

Microwave tip: In 2-cup measure, combine juice, broth, cornstarch, sugar and thyme. Microwave at High for 2½ to 4½ minutes, or until sauce is thickened and translucent, stirring once or twice. Continue as directed.

Nutrition Facts

Serving Size
1 fillet (143g)
Servings
per Recipe 4
Calories 114
Calories
from Fat 19

Amount/serving	%DV*	Amount/serving	%DV*
Total Fat 2g	3%	Total Carbohydrate 6g	2%
Saturated Fat <1g	1%	Dietary Fiber <1g	0%
Cholesterol 23mg	8%	Sugars 4g	
Sodium 136mg	6%	Protein 17g	

Vitamin A 2% • Vitamin C 20% • Calcium 4% • Iron 2%
*Percent Daily Values (DV) are based on a 2000 calorie diet.

Menu Planning Guide
One serving of this recipe provides:
  1 Meat, Poultry & Fish

Diet Exchanges:
3 lean meat

Fish & Seafood

SAFFRON SHRIMP & TOMATO

1 can (14½ oz.) ready-to-serve
    chicken broth, defatted*
½ cup water
1 cup uncooked converted white rice
½ cup coarsely chopped green pepper
⅓ cup chopped onion
    Dash ground saffron
20 cooked medium shrimp, shelled and deveined
    (about ½ lb.)
1 medium tomato, seeded and coarsely chopped
    (1 cup)

6 servings

*Defat broth by chilling 4 hours; skim and discard
solidified fat from surface.

1 Bring broth and water to boil over high heat in 2-quart saucepan. Stir in rice, green pepper, onion and saffron. Return to boil. Cover. Reduce heat to low. Simmer for 20 to 25 minutes, or until rice is tender and liquid is absorbed.

2 Stir in shrimp. Increase heat to medium-low. Cook for 2 to 3 minutes, or until shrimp is hot, stirring occasionally. Stir in tomato.

Nutrition Facts	Amount/serving	%DV*	Amount/serving	%DV*
Serving Size approximately 1 cup (214g) Servings per Recipe 6	Total Fat <1g	1%	Total Carbohydrate 22g	7%
	Saturated Fat <1g	1%	Dietary Fiber <1g	3%
Calories 129 Calories from Fat 5	Cholesterol 39mg	13%	Sugars 2g	
	Sodium 266mg	11%	Protein 8g	

Vitamin A 4% • Vitamin C 20% • Calcium 2% • Iron 10%
*Percent Daily Values (DV) are based on a 2000 calorie diet.

Menu Planning Guide
One serving of this recipe provides:
½ Vegetable
1 Bread, Cereal, Rice & Pasta

Diet Exchanges:
½ lean meat • 1 starch • ½ vegetable

FILLET OF SOLE ALMONDINE

4 thin red onion slices
6 thin lemon slices
¼ cup sliced green onions
2 tablespoons sliced almonds
2 fillets sole or other lean, white fish (4 oz. each),
    ½ inch thick

⅛ teaspoon salt
⅛ teaspoon white or lemon pepper
    Paprika

2 servings

1 Heat oven to 350°F. Spray 12 x 8-inch baking dish with nonstick vegetable cooking spray. Arrange 2 slices each of red onion and lemon in dish. Sprinkle with half of green onions and 1 tablespoon almonds.

2 Arrange fillets in single layer over onions, lemon and almonds. Sprinkle lightly with salt, pepper and paprika. Top with remaining red onion, lemon, green onions and almonds. Cover dish with foil. Bake for 25 to 28 minutes, or until fish is firm and opaque and just begins to flake.

Nutrition Facts	Amount/serving	%DV*	Amount/serving	%DV*
Serving Size 1 fillet (160g)	Total Fat 6g	9%	Total Carbohydrate 7g	2%
Servings per Recipe 2	Saturated Fat <1g	4%	Dietary Fiber 2g	8%
Calories 175	Cholesterol 60mg	20%	Sugars 4g	
Calories from Fat 53	Sodium 230mg	10%	Protein 24g	

Vitamin A 2% • Vitamin C 30% • Calcium 6% • Iron 6%
*Percent Daily Values (DV) are based on a 2000 calorie diet.

Menu Planning Guide
One serving of this recipe provides:
  1 Meat, Poultry & Fish
  ½ Vegetable

Diet Exchanges:
3 lean meat • ½ vegetable

SWORDFISH WITH CREOLE RELISH

½ cup chopped seeded tomato
¼ cup chopped red pepper
¼ cup finely chopped celery
¼ cup finely chopped onion
1 tablespoon plus 1 teaspoon lemon juice, divided
1 clove garlic, minced
1 teaspoon vegetable oil
½ teaspoon dried oregano leaves

¼ teaspoon dried basil leaves
¼ teaspoon dried thyme leaves
¼ teaspoon sugar
⅛ teaspoon salt
3 to 5 drops red pepper sauce
2 swordfish or halibut steaks (8 oz. each),
    about 1 inch thick

4 servings

1 Combine tomato and red pepper in blender. Process until nearly smooth. Set aside. Spray 7-inch nonstick skillet with nonstick vegetable cooking spray. Place celery, onion, 1 teaspoon juice, the garlic and oil in skillet. Cook over medium heat for 5 to 7 minutes, or until vegetables are tender-crisp, stirring frequently. Stir in tomato mixture and remaining ingredients, except swordfish and remaining juice. Cook for 3 to 4 minutes, or until liquid is reduced and relish thickens, stirring frequently. Remove from heat. Cover to keep warm. Set relish aside.

2 Cut each steak in half crosswise to yield 4 serving-size pieces. Spray broiler pan with nonstick vegetable cooking spray. Arrange steaks on rack in broiler pan. Sprinkle steaks evenly with remaining 1 tablespoon juice.

3 Place under broiler with surface of steaks 4 to 6 inches from heat. Broil for 4 to 6 minutes, or until fish is firm and opaque and just begins to flake. Serve each steak with about 3 tablespoons relish.

Nutrition Facts	Amount/serving	%DV*	Amount/serving	%DV*
Serving Size ½ steak (150g)	Total Fat 6g	9%	Total Carbohydrate 4g	1%
Servings per Recipe 4	Saturated Fat 1g	7%	Dietary Fiber <1g	4%
Calories 165	Cholesterol 44mg	15%	Sugars 3g	
Calories from Fat 53	Sodium 179mg	7%	Protein 23g	

Vitamin A 8% • Vitamin C 25% • Calcium 2% • Iron 8%
*Percent Daily Values (DV) are based on a 2000 calorie diet.

Menu Planning Guide
One serving of this recipe provides:
1 Meat, Poultry & Fish
½ Vegetable

Diet Exchanges:
3 lean meat • ½ vegetable

SCALLOPS WITH WINE & CHEESE SAUCE

1   cup water
1   lb. bay scallops, rinsed and drained
3/4 cup shredded low-fat Swiss cheese
1   tablespoon all-purpose flour
1/2 cup dry white wine
2   teaspoons margarine
1/2 teaspoon dry mustard
1/2 teaspoon garlic powder, divided

1/4 cup chopped seeded tomato
1   tablespoon snipped fresh parsley
1   tablespoon sliced green onion
1   teaspoon fresh lemon juice
3   English muffins, split and toasted
     Freshly ground pepper

6 servings

1 Place water in 10-inch non-stick skillet. Bring to boil over high heat. Add scallops. Cook for 2½ to 4 minutes, or until scallops are firm and opaque, stirring occasionally. Drain. Set aside. In medium plastic food-storage bag, combine cheese and flour. Shake to coat. Set aside.

2 Combine wine, margarine, mustard and ¼ teaspoon garlic powder in 2-quart saucepan. Bring to boil over medium heat. Stir in cheese mixture. Cook for 30 to 45 seconds, or until cheese melts, stirring constantly. Stir in scallops. Cook for 1 to 2 minutes, or until hot, stirring frequently. Remove from heat.

3 Combine tomato, parsley, onion, juice and remaining ¼ teaspoon garlic powder in small mixing bowl. Spoon scallops and cheese sauce evenly over English muffin halves. Top evenly with tomato mixture. Sprinkle each serving with dash of pepper.

Nutrition Facts	Amount/serving	%DV*	Amount/serving	%DV*
Serving Size ½ muffin (115g) Servings per Recipe 6 Calories 194 Calories from Fat 60	Total Fat 7g	10%	Total Carbohydrate 17g	6%
	Saturated Fat 3g	14%	Dietary Fiber 1g	4%
	Cholesterol 29mg	10%	Sugars 1g	
	Sodium 275mg	11%	Protein 16g	

Vitamin A 8% • Vitamin C 8% • Calcium 20% • Iron 6%
*Percent Daily Values (DV) are based on a 2000 calorie diet.

Menu Planning Guide
One serving of this recipe provides:
1 Meat, Poultry & Fish
1 Bread, Cereal, Rice & Pasta

Diet Exchanges:
2 lean meat • 1 starch

CHINESE-STYLE FISH WITH VEGETABLES

½ oz. dried shiitake mushrooms

1½ cups hot water

1½ lbs. cod fillets, cut into 1-inch pieces

½ teaspoon salt

1 egg white, beaten

3 tablespoons cornstarch

Sauce:

1¼ cups reserved mushroom liquid

2 tablespoons low-sodium soy sauce

1 tablespoon rice wine vinegar

1 tablespoon dry sherry

1 tablespoon plus 1 teaspoon cornstarch

1 tablespoon sugar

1 teaspoon instant chicken bouillon granules

½ teaspoon sesame oil

½ cup water

1 tablespoon vegetable oil

1 clove garlic, minced

1 teaspoon grated fresh gingerroot

1 medium green pepper, cut into 1-inch pieces

1 medium red pepper, cut into 1-inch pieces

1 medium carrot, cut into 2 x ¼-inch strips
(¾ cup)

1 small onion, cut into 12 wedges

½ cup diagonally sliced green onions
(1½-inch lengths)

4 cups hot cooked white rice

8 servings

1 Place mushrooms in small mixing bowl. Pour hot water over mushrooms. Let soak for 30 minutes, or until softened. Drain liquid, reserving 1¼ cups. Slice mushrooms. Set aside.

2 Place fish in medium mixing bowl. Sprinkle with salt. Add egg white. Stir to coat. Sprinkle 3 tablespoons cornstarch over fish mixture. Toss to coat. Set aside.

3 Combine sauce ingredients in small mixing bowl. Set aside. In wok, heat ½ cup water over medium-high heat until boiling. Spray round cooking rack with nonstick vegetable cooking spray. Arrange fish on prepared rack. Set rack in wok about 1½ inches above water. Cover. Steam for 3 to 5 minutes, or until fish is firm and opaque and just begins to flake. Remove from heat. Set aside.

4 Drain and discard water from wok. Wipe wok with paper towel. In same wok, heat vegetable oil over high heat. Add garlic and gingerroot. Stir in prepared mushrooms and remaining ingredients, except rice. Cook for 3 to 4 minutes, or until onion is tender-crisp, stirring constantly. Add fish. Cook for 1 to 2 minutes, or until hot, stirring gently. Add sauce mixture. Cook for 1 to 2 minutes, or until sauce is thickened and translucent, stirring constantly. Serve over rice.

Nutrition Facts	Amount/serving	%DV*	Amount/serving	%DV*
Serving Size 1¼ cups (265g)	Total Fat 3g	4%	Total Carbohydrate 40g	13%
Servings per Recipe 8	Saturated Fat <1g	0%	Dietary Fiber 1g	4%
Calories 266	Cholesterol 36mg	12%	Sugars 3g	
Calories from Fat 26	Sodium 451mg	19%	Protein 19g	
	Vitamin A 35% • Vitamin C 40% • Calcium 4% • Iron 10%			
	*Percent Daily Values (DV) are based on a 2000 calorie diet.			

Menu Planning Guide

One serving of this recipe provides:

1 Meat, Poultry & Fish
1 Vegetable
2 Bread, Cereal, Rice & Pasta

Diet Exchanges:

2 lean meat • 2 starch • 1 vegetable

SPICY MANHATTAN CLAM CHOWDER

1 cup cubed red potatoes (1/4-inch cubes)

1/3 cup chopped onion

1/4 cup grated carrot

1/4 cup water

1 tablespoon margarine

2 cans (14 1/2 oz. each) whole tomatoes, undrained, cut up

1 can (6 1/2 oz.) minced clams, undrained

3/4 cup spicy vegetable juice

2 tablespoons catsup ◆

2 tablespoons snipped fresh parsley

1 bay leaf

1/4 to 1/2 teaspoon red pepper sauce

1/4 teaspoon dried thyme leaves

1/8 teaspoon pepper

6 servings

1 Combine potatoes, onion, carrot, water and margarine in 3-quart saucepan. Cook over medium heat for 8 to 10 minutes, or until vegetables are tender, stirring frequently. (If vegetables begin to stick, add additional 1/4 cup water and continue cooking.)

2 Stir in remaining ingredients. Bring mixture to boil over high heat. Cover. Reduce heat to low. Simmer for 10 to 15 minutes, or until chowder is hot and flavors are blended, stirring occasionally. Remove and discard bay leaf before serving.

Microwave tip: Omit water. In 2-quart casserole, combine potatoes, onion, carrot and margarine. Cover. Microwave at High for 5 to 6 minutes, or until vegetables are tender, stirring once. Stir in remaining ingredients. Re-cover. Microwave at 70% (Medium High) for 10 to 14 minutes, or until chowder is hot and flavors are blended, stirring once. Remove and discard bay leaf before serving.

◆ Look for Healthy Choice® products at your favorite supermarket.

Nutrition Facts	Amount/serving	%DV*	Amount/serving	%DV*
Serving Size approximately 1 cup (254g)	Total Fat 3g	4%	Total Carbohydrate 16g	5%
Servings per Recipe 6	Saturated Fat <1g	2%	Dietary Fiber 2g	8%
Calories 106	Cholesterol 10mg	3%	Sugars 6g	
Calories from Fat 24	Sodium 451mg	19%	Protein 6g	

Vitamin A 60% • Vitamin C 60% • Calcium 6% • Iron 35%

*Percent Daily Values (DV) are based on a 2000 calorie diet.

Menu Planning Guide
One serving of this recipe provides:
1 1/2 Vegetable

Diet Exchanges:
1/2 lean meat • 1/2 starch • 1 vegetable

VEGETABLES

TAMALE PIE

Filling:
1 can (16 oz.) whole tomatoes, drained and cut up
2 cups frozen corn
1 can (15 oz.) pinto beans, rinsed and drained
1 can (4 oz.) chopped green chilies
⅓ cup chopped green pepper
⅓ cup chopped onion
½ teaspoon ground cumin
½ teaspoon chili powder
¼ teaspoon dried cilantro leaves
¼ teaspoon dried oregano leaves
¼ teaspoon garlic powder

Crust:
¼ cup yellow cornmeal

½ cup all-purpose flour
1 teaspoon baking powder
1 tablespoon sugar
¼ teaspoon salt
½ cup skim milk
¼ cup frozen cholesterol-free egg product ◆,
    defrosted, or 1 egg
1 tablespoon vegetable oil

6 servings

1 Heat oven to 350°F. In 3-quart saucepan, combine filling ingredients. Cook over medium heat for 10 to 15 minutes, or until mixture is very hot and flavors are blended, stirring occasionally. Cover to keep warm. Set aside.

2 Combine cornmeal, flour, baking powder, sugar and salt in small mixing bowl. Add remaining ingredients. Mix just until batter is blended.

3 Spoon filling into 9-inch round cake dish. Spoon batter over filling. Sprinkle top with paprika, if desired.

4 Bake for 30 to 40 minutes, or until cornmeal crust is golden brown. Let stand for 10 minutes. Garnish with fresh red chili pepper or jalapeño pepper, if desired.

◆ Look for Healthy Choice® products at your favorite supermarket.

Nutrition Facts	Amount/serving	%DV*	Amount/serving	%DV*
Serving Size ⅙ pie (276g)	Total Fat 3g	5%	Total Carbohydrate 53g	18%
Servings per Recipe 6	Saturated Fat <1g	2%	Dietary Fiber 9g	37%
Calories 273	Cholesterol <1mg	0%	Sugars 8g	
Calories from Fat 29	Sodium 380mg	16%	Protein 11g	

Vitamin A 10% • Vitamin C 35% • Calcium 15% • Iron 20%
*Percent Daily Values (DV) are based on a 2000 calorie diet.

Menu Planning Guide
One serving of this recipe provides:
½ Meat, Poultry & Fish
1 Vegetable
1 Bread, Cereal, Rice & Pasta

Diet Exchanges:
3 starch • 1 vegetable

SWEET-SPICED BRUSSELS SPROUTS & APPLES

1   tablespoon honey
⅛   teaspoon ground nutmeg
2   cups water
1   lb. fresh Brussels sprouts, trimmed and
      cut in half
1   medium red cooking apple, cored and cut
      into ½-inch cubes (1½ cups)
1   teaspoon margarine

4 servings

1 Combine honey and nutmeg in small bowl. Set aside. In 2-quart saucepan, bring water to boil over high heat. Add sprouts. Return to boil. Cover.

2 Reduce heat to medium-low. Cook for 5 to 7 minutes, or until sprouts are tender. Drain. Add honey mixture, apple and margarine. Mix well. Cover. Let stand for 5 minutes, or until apple is hot.

Microwave tip: Reduce water to ¼ cup. In 2-quart casserole, combine sprouts and water. Cover. Microwave at High for 6 to 8 minutes, or until tender-crisp, stirring once or twice. Drain. Add honey mixture, apple and margarine. Mix well. Re-cover. Microwave at High for 1½ to 3 minutes, or until sprouts are tender and apple is hot.

Nutrition Facts	Amount/serving	%DV*	Amount/serving	%DV*
Serving Size ¾ cup (154g)	Total Fat 2g	3%	Total Carbohydrate 20g	7%
	Saturated Fat <1g	2%	Dietary Fiber 6g	23%
Servings per Recipe 4	Cholesterol 0mg	0%	Sugars 13g	
Calories 90	Sodium 35mg	1%	Protein 3g	
Calories from Fat 15	Vitamin A 10% • Vitamin C 120% • Calcium 4% • Iron 8%			
	*Percent Daily Values (DV) are based on a 2000 calorie diet.			

Menu Planning Guide
One serving of this recipe provides:
  1 Vegetable

Diet Exchanges:
1 starch • 1 vegetable • 1 fruit

RATATOUILLE WITH POTATOES

2 cups water
8 oz. new potatoes, cut into ¾-inch cubes
    (1½ cups)
1 tablespoon olive oil
1 small red onion, chopped (½ cup)
2 cloves garlic, minced
1 small eggplant (10 oz.), cut into 1-inch
    chunks (4 cups)
8 oz. fresh mushrooms, sliced (3 cups)
3 Roma tomatoes, cut into 1-inch chunks
    (1½ cups)
1 medium green pepper, cut into 1-inch chunks
    (1 cup)
1 medium zucchini, sliced (1 cup)
½ teaspoon dried basil leaves

½ teaspoon dried thyme leaves
½ teaspoon dried oregano leaves
½ teaspoon salt
¼ teaspoon freshly ground pepper
¼ cup shredded fresh Parmesan cheese (optional)

6 servings

1 Place water in 8-quart stockpot. Bring to boil over high heat. Add potatoes. Return to boil. Cover. Reduce heat to medium-low. Cook for 10 to 11 minutes, or until potatoes are tender. Drain. Remove potatoes from pot. Set aside.

2 Place oil in same pot. Heat over medium heat. Add onion and garlic. Cook for 2½ to 3 minutes, or until onion is tender-crisp, stirring frequently.

3 Add remaining ingredients, except cheese. Cook for 6 to 8 minutes, or until eggplant, zucchini and tomatoes are tender, stirring frequently.

4 Add potatoes. Cook for 1 to 1½ minutes, or until hot, stirring occasionally. Sprinkle each serving evenly with cheese.

Nutrition Facts	Amount/serving	%DV*	Amount/serving	%DV*	Menu Planning Guide
Serving Size 1 cup (261g)	Total Fat 3g	4%	Total Carbohydrate 21g	7%	One serving of this recipe provides:
Servings per Recipe 6	Saturated Fat <1g	2%	Dietary Fiber 5g	19%	3 Vegetable
Calories 115	Cholesterol 0mg	0%	Sugars 6g		
Calories from Fat 25	Sodium 190mg	8%	Protein 4g		

Vitamin A 6% • Vitamin C 70% • Calcium 4% • Iron 10%

*Percent Daily Values (DV) are based on a 2000 calorie diet.

Diet Exchanges:
1 starch • 1 vegetable

BEANS WITH RED PEPPER PURÉE

1 large red pepper, seeded and cut into 1-inch
  chunks (1⅓ cups)
3¼ cups water, divided
1 clove garlic, minced
½ teaspoon red wine vinegar
½ teaspoon salt
¼ teaspoon instant chicken bouillon granules
¼ teaspoon dried oregano leaves
⅛ teaspoon pepper
½ lb. fresh green beans
½ lb. fresh wax beans

8 servings

1 Combine red pepper, ¼ cup water, the garlic, vinegar, salt, bouillon, oregano and pepper in 1-quart saucepan. Bring to boil over medium-high heat. Cover. Reduce heat to low. Simmer for 14 to 16 minutes, or until pepper is very tender. Drain. In food processor or blender, process mixture until smooth. Cover to keep warm. Set red pepper purée aside.

2 Combine beans and remaining 3 cups water in 3-quart saucepan. Bring to boil over medium-high heat. Reduce heat to low. Simmer, uncovered, for 5 minutes. Cover. Cook for 8 to 10 minutes, or until tender. Drain. Arrange beans on serving platter. Spoon purée over beans.

Nutrition Facts	Amount/serving	%DV*	Amount/serving	%DV*
Serving Size approximately ½ cup (157g)	Total Fat <1g	0%	Total Carbohydrate 5g	2%
Servings per Recipe 8	Saturated Fat <1g	0%	Dietary Fiber 1g	5%
Calories 23	Cholesterol 0mg	0%	Sugars 2g	
Calories from Fat 2	Sodium 166mg	7%	Protein 1g	
	Vitamin A 8% • Vitamin C 60% • Calcium 2% • Iron 4%			
	*Percent Daily Values (DV) are based on a 2000 calorie diet.			

Menu Planning Guide
One serving of this recipe provides:
1 Vegetable

Diet Exchanges:
1 vegetable

SPICY MOROCCAN VEGETABLES

1 medium onion, chopped (1 cup)

1 medium turnip, cut into ¼-inch cubes (1 cup)

2 medium carrots, thinly sliced (1 cup)

2 tablespoons olive oil

2 cloves garlic, minced

1½ teaspoons ground cumin

½ teaspoon pepper

¼ teaspoon salt

1 medium red pepper, seeded and cut into 1-inch chunks (1 cup)

1 medium zucchini, thinly sliced (1 cup)

1 can (16 oz.) garbanzo beans, rinsed and drained

1 cup raisins

3 tablespoons snipped fresh parsley

6 servings

1 Combine onion, turnip, carrots, oil, garlic, cumin, pepper and salt in 10-inch nonstick skillet. Cook over medium-high heat for 6 to 7 minutes, or until vegetables are tender-crisp, stirring occasionally.

2 Stir in red pepper and zucchini. Cook for 2 to 3 minutes, or until tender-crisp, stirring occasionally. Stir in beans, raisins and parsley. Cook for 2 to 3 minutes, or until hot, stirring occasionally.

Nutrition Facts	Amount/serving	%DV*	Amount/serving	%DV*
Serving Size approximately ½ cup (209g) Servings per Recipe 6 Calories 258 Calories from Fat 59	Total Fat 7g	10%	Total Carbohydrate 46g	15%
	Saturated Fat <1g	4%	Dietary Fiber 7g	30%
	Cholesterol 0mg	0%	Sugars 24g	
	Sodium 123mg	5%	Protein 8g	
	Vitamin A 80% • Vitamin C 80% • Calcium 8% • Iron 20%			
	*Percent Daily Values (DV) are based on a 2000 calorie diet.			

Menu Planning Guide
One serving of this recipe provides:
1 Vegetable
1 Fruit

Diet Exchanges:
1½ starch • 1 vegetable • 1 fruit • 1 fat

SUMMER SQUASH SCRAMBLE

1 *medium onion, coarsely chopped (1 cup)*

1 *clove garlic, minced*

2 *teaspoons olive oil*

2 *medium zucchini squash, cut into ¼-inch*
   slices (2 cups)

1 *medium yellow squash, cut into ¼-inch*
   slices (1 cup)

½ *teaspoon dried basil leaves*

¼ *teaspoon salt*

2 *medium tomatoes, chopped (2 cups)*

1 *to 2 tablespoons grated Parmesan cheese*
   (optional)

8 servings

1 Combine onion, garlic and oil in 10-inch nonstick skillet. Cook over medium-high heat for 2 to 3 minutes, or until onion is tender, stirring frequently.

2 Add squashes, basil and salt. Cook for 5 to 7 minutes, or until squashes are tender-crisp, stirring constantly.

3 Stir in tomatoes. Cook for 1 to 2 minutes, or until hot, stirring constantly. Remove from heat. Sprinkle with Parmesan cheese.

Nutrition Facts	Amount/serving	%DV*	Amount/serving	%DV*
Serving Size approximately ½ cup (103g)	Total Fat 1g	2%	Total Carbohydrate 6g	2%
Servings per Recipe 8	Saturated Fat <1g	1%	Dietary Fiber 1g	4%
Calories 37	Cholesterol 0mg	0%	Sugars 3g	
Calories from Fat 12	Sodium 72mg	3%	Protein 1g	
	Vitamin A 15% • Vitamin C 25% • Calcium 2% • Iron 2%			
	*Percent Daily Values (DV) are based on a 2000 calorie diet.			

Menu Planning Guide
One serving of this recipe provides:
1 Vegetable

Diet Exchanges:
1 vegetable

164

SPINACH-STUFFED PEPPERS

3 green, red or yellow peppers
8 cups water
1 pkg. (10 oz.) frozen chopped spinach
1 medium tomato, seeded and chopped (1 cup)
1 small onion, chopped (½ cup)
⅓ cup unseasoned dry bread crumbs

½ teaspoon salt
½ teaspoon pepper
¼ teaspoon garlic powder
¼ cup shredded nonfat or part-skim
    mozzarella cheese ◆

6 servings

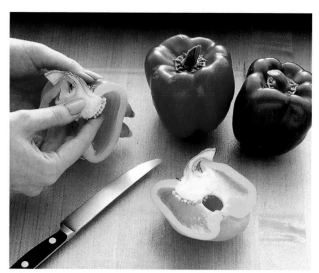

1 Cut each pepper in half lengthwise. Remove seeds. In 6-quart Dutch oven or stockpot, bring water to boil over high heat. Add peppers. Cook for 4 to 5 minutes, or until tender-crisp. Rinse with cold water. Drain. Arrange peppers cut-sides-up in 10-inch square casserole. Set aside.

2 Heat oven to 350°F. Prepare spinach as directed on package. Drain, pressing to remove excess moisture. In small mixing bowl, combine spinach and remaining ingredients, except cheese. Spoon spinach mixture evenly into peppers. Sprinkle cheese evenly over peppers. Bake for 25 to 30 minutes, or until cheese is melted and peppers are hot through center.

Microwave tip: Reduce water to ¼ cup. In 10-inch square casserole, arrange peppers cut-sides-up. Sprinkle with water. Cover with plastic wrap. Microwave at High for 6 to 8 minutes, or until tender-crisp, rearranging once. Drain. Continue as directed.

◆ Look for Healthy Choice® products at your favorite supermarket.

Nutrition Facts	Amount/serving	%DV*	Amount/serving	%DV*
Serving Size ½ pepper (118g)	Total Fat <1g	1%	Total Carbohydrate 11g	4%
Servings per Recipe 6	Saturated Fat <1g	1%	Dietary Fiber 2g	8%
Calories 60	Cholesterol <1mg	0%	Sugars 3g	
Calories from Fat 5	Sodium 293mg	12%	Protein 4g	

Vitamin A 60% • Vitamin C 60% • Calcium 8% • Iron 6%
*Percent Daily Values (DV) are based on a 2000 calorie diet.

Menu Planning Guide
One serving of this recipe provides:
2 Vegetable

Diet Exchanges:
2 vegetable

DIXIE VEGETABLE DISH

1 can (16 oz.) black-eyed peas, rinsed and drained
1 pkg. (10 oz.) frozen corn, defrosted
1 medium tomato, seeded and chopped (1 cup)
1 medium zucchini, cut lengthwise into quarters,
    then sliced crosswise (1 cup)
¼ cup water
1½ teaspoons snipped fresh basil leaves or
    ½ teaspoon dried basil leaves
¼ teaspoon salt

6 servings

1 Combine all ingredients in 2-quart saucepan. Cover. Cook over high heat for 5 to 7 minutes, or until vegetables are hot and flavors are blended, stirring occasionally. Drain.

Microwave tip: Omit water. In 2-quart casserole, combine all ingredients. Cover. Microwave at High for 7 to 10 minutes, or until vegetables are hot and flavors are blended, stirring once or twice.

Nutrition Facts	Amount/serving	%DV*	Amount/serving	%DV*
Serving Size approximately ½ cup (164g) Servings per Recipe 6	Total Fat <1g	0%	Total Carbohydrate 24g	8%
	Saturated Fat <1g	0%	Dietary Fiber 5g	20%
	Cholesterol 0mg	0%	Sugars 4g	
Calories 108 Calories from Fat 3	Sodium 97mg	4%	Protein 4g	

Vitamin A 15% • Vitamin C 15% • Calcium 10% • Iron 6%
*Percent Daily Values (DV) are based on a 2000 calorie diet.

Menu Planning Guide
One serving of this recipe provides:
1 Vegetable

Diet Exchanges:
1½ starch

ORANGE-GINGERED ACORN SQUASH

1 acorn squash (about 1½ lbs.)
1 tablespoon frozen orange juice concentrate, defrosted
1 tablespoon honey
½ teaspoon ground ginger

¼ cup water
    Ground cinnamon
2 slices orange, quartered

4 servings

1 Heat oven to 350°F. Cut squash lengthwise into quarters. Remove seeds. Arrange quarters cut-sides-up in 10-inch square casserole. Pierce cut side of each quarter in several places with fork.

2 Combine concentrate, honey and ginger in small bowl. Brush juice mixture evenly over quarters.

3 Pour water into bottom of casserole. Cover. Bake for 40 to 45 minutes, or until squash is tender. Let stand, covered, for 5 minutes. To serve, sprinkle lightly with cinnamon and garnish with quartered orange slices.

Microwave tip: Prepare as directed, except omit water. Microwave, covered, at High for 8 to 10 minutes, or until squash is tender, rotating casserole once.

Nutrition Facts	Amount/serving	%DV*	Amount/serving	%DV*
Serving Size ¼ squash (153g)	Total Fat <1g	0%	Total Carbohydrate 27g	9%
Servings per Recipe 4	Saturated Fat <1g	0%	Dietary Fiber 6g	24%
Calories 103	Cholesterol 0mg	0%	Sugars 11g	
Calories from Fat 2	Sodium 6mg	0%	Protein 2g	

Vitamin A 10% • Vitamin C 40% • Calcium 6% • Iron 8%
*Percent Daily Values (DV) are based on a 2000 calorie diet.

Menu Planning Guide
One serving of this recipe provides:
1 Vegetable

Diet Exchanges:
1½ starch

HERBED ARTICHOKES

2   *fresh artichokes (10 to 12 oz. each)*
14 *cups water*
¼   *teaspoon fresh lemon peel*
1   *tablespoon fresh lemon juice*

2   *teaspoons margarine, melted*
½   *teaspoon dry mustard*
1   *tablespoon snipped fresh chives*

4 servings

1 Trim each artichoke stem close to base. Cut 1 inch off tops. Trim ends off each leaf.

2 Cut each artichoke lengthwise into quarters. Remove some of center leaves and scrape out choke from each piece. Discard choke. Bring water to boil over high heat in 6-quart Dutch oven or stockpot. Add artichoke quarters. Cook for 7 to 9 minutes, or until tender. Drain.

3 Combine peel, juice, margarine and mustard in small bowl. Drizzle juice mixture over artichoke quarters, making sure to get mixture between leaves. Sprinkle chives evenly over quarters.

Nutrition Facts	Amount/serving	%DV*	Amount/serving	%DV*
Serving Size ½ artichoke (64g)	Total Fat 2g	3%	Total Carbohydrate 6g	2%
Servings per Recipe 4	Saturated Fat <1g	2%	Dietary Fiber 3g	12%
Calories 46	Cholesterol 0mg	0%	Sugars 2g	
Calories from Fat 19	Sodium 76mg	3%	Protein 2g	

Vitamin A 4% • Vitamin C 15% • Calcium 2% • Iron 4%
*Percent Daily Values (DV) are based on a 2000 calorie diet.

Menu Planning Guide
One serving of this recipe provides:
1 Vegetable

Diet Exchanges:
1 vegetable • ½ fat

SPICY GLAZED CARROTS

1   pkg. (16 oz.) frozen crinkle-cut carrots
¼   cup apricot preserves
2   tablespoons water
¼   teaspoon chili powder
¼   teaspoon salt
⅛   teaspoon ground ginger
    Dash cayenne

6 servings

1 Combine all ingredients in 2-quart saucepan. Cover. Cook over medium heat for 12 to 17 minutes, or until carrots are hot, stirring occasionally.

Microwave tip: Combine all ingredients in 2-quart casserole. Cover. Microwave at High for 7 to 10 minutes, or until carrots are hot, stirring twice.

Nutrition Facts	Amount/serving	%DV*	Amount/serving	%DV*
Serving Size approximately ½ cup (80g)	Total Fat <1g	0%	Total Carbohydrate 14g	5%
Servings per Recipe 6	Saturated Fat 0g	0%	Dietary Fiber 2g	8%
	Cholesterol 0mg	0%	Sugars 11g	
Calories 55	Sodium 132mg	6%	Protein <1g	
Calories from Fat 1	Vitamin A 220% • Vitamin C 4% • Calcium 2% • Iron 2%			
	*Percent Daily Values (DV) are based on a 2000 calorie diet.			

Menu Planning Guide
One serving of this recipe provides:
1   Vegetable

Diet Exchanges:
½ starch • 1 vegetable

COLORFUL MARINATED VEGETABLES

3 medium zucchini, cut into ½-inch slices
     (5 cups)
2 medium carrots, cut into ¼-inch slices (1 cup)
½ cup thinly sliced onion, separated into rings
½ cup coarsely chopped red pepper
½ cup water
¼ cup spicy vegetable juice
2 tablespoons white wine vinegar
2 tablespoons fresh lemon juice
1 tablespoon snipped fresh parsley
1 clove garlic, minced
1 teaspoon sugar
¼ teaspoon celery seed
¼ teaspoon salt

12 servings

1 Combine zucchini, carrots, onion, pepper and water in 3-quart saucepan. Cover. Cook over high heat for 5 to 7 minutes, or until vegetables are tender-crisp, stirring occasionally. Drain. Set aside.

2 Combine remaining ingredients in 1-cup measure. In large mixing bowl or salad bowl, combine vegetable mixture and juice mixture. Toss to coat. Cover with plastic wrap. Chill at least 4 hours, stirring occasionally. Serve with slotted spoon.

Nutrition Facts	Amount/serving	%DV*	Amount/serving	%DV*
Serving Size approximately ½ cup (61g)	Total Fat <1g	0%	Total Carbohydrate 4g	1%
Servings per Recipe 12	Saturated Fat <1g	0%	Dietary Fiber 1g	4%
Calories 15	Cholesterol 0mg	0%	Sugars 2g	
Calories from Fat 1	Sodium 69mg	3%	Protein 1g	

Vitamin A 45% • Vitamin C 25% • Calcium 2% • Iron 2%
*Percent Daily Values (DV) are based on a 2000 calorie diet.

Menu Planning Guide
One serving of this recipe provides:
1 Vegetable

Diet Exchanges:
1 vegetable

PASTA, RICE & BEANS

HOT PASTA SALAD

2 tablespoons balsamic vinegar

2 teaspoons olive oil

⅛ teaspoon salt

1 medium green pepper, cut into ¼-inch strips

½ medium red onion, cut in half lengthwise and
   thinly sliced (1 cup)

2 teaspoons poppy seed

2 cups hot cooked linguine (6 oz. uncooked)

1 medium tomato, cut into thin wedges

4 servings

1 In small bowl, combine vinegar, oil and salt. Set aside.

2 Spray 12-inch nonstick skillet with nonstick vegetable cooking spray. Heat skillet over medium heat. Add pepper, onion and poppy seed. Cook for 4 to 6 minutes, or until vegetables are tender, stirring frequently. Reduce heat to medium-low. Add linguine and tomato. Cook for 1 to 1½ minutes, or until hot, stirring frequently. Add vinegar mixture. Toss to combine. Serve hot.

Nutrition Facts	Amount/serving	%DV*	Amount/serving	%DV*
Serving Size ½ cup (206g)	Total Fat 4g	6%	Total Carbohydrate 36g	12%
Servings per Recipe 4	Saturated Fat <1g	2%	Dietary Fiber 3g	13%
Calories 201	Cholesterol 0mg	0%	Sugars 4g	
Calories from Fat 33	Sodium 72mg	3%	Protein 6g	

Vitamin A 4% • Vitamin C 60% • Calcium 4% • Iron 10%
*Percent Daily Values (DV) are based on a 2000 calorie diet.

Menu Planning Guide
One serving of this recipe provides:
1 Vegetable
1 Bread, Cereal, Rice & Pasta

Diet Exchanges:
2 starch • 1 vegetable

BROWN RICE WITH TOASTED PINE NUTS

3½ cups water, divided
1 cup uncooked long-grain brown rice
1 clove garlic, minced
1 teaspoon instant chicken bouillon
    granules
½ teaspoon salt
⅛ teaspoon pepper
¼ cup pine nuts
2 medium carrots, finely chopped (¾ cup)

¼ cup snipped fresh parsley
2 tablespoons sliced green onion

6 servings

1 Combine 3 cups water, the rice, garlic, bouillon, salt and pepper in 3-quart saucepan. Bring to boil over high heat. Cover. Reduce heat to low. Cook for 50 minutes, or until liquid is absorbed and rice is tender. (Do not remove cover during cooking.)

2 Heat oven to 400°F. In 8-inch square baking pan, bake pine nuts for 4 to 5 minutes, or until light golden brown, stirring twice. Set aside.

3 Place remaining ½ cup water in 1-quart saucepan. Bring to boil over medium heat. Add carrots. Cook for 2½ to 4 minutes, or until tender-crisp, stirring occasionally. Drain. In medium mixing bowl, combine rice, pine nuts, carrots, parsley and onion. Serve hot.

Microwave tip: Reduce water to 3 cups plus 2 tablespoons. Prepare recipe as directed, except combine carrots and remaining 2 tablespoons water in 1-quart casserole. Cover. Microwave at High for 3 to 4 minutes, or until carrots are tender-crisp, stirring once. Continue as directed.

Nutrition Facts

Serving Size ½ cup (127g)
Servings per Recipe 6
Calories 154
Calories from Fat 40

Amount/serving	%DV*	Amount/serving	%DV*
Total Fat 4g	7%	Total Carbohydrate 26g	9%
Saturated Fat 1g	4%	Dietary Fiber 3g	11%
Cholesterol 0mg	0%	Sugars 2g	
Sodium 346mg	14%	Protein 4g	

Vitamin A 45% • Vitamin C 8% • Calcium 2% • Iron 8%
*Percent Daily Values (DV) are based on a 2000 calorie diet.

Menu Planning Guide

One serving of this recipe provides:
1½ Bread, Cereal, Rice & Pasta

Diet Exchanges:

1½ starch

ROSEMARY NEW POTATOES & BEANS

2 cups water
1 lb. new potatoes, thinly sliced (3 cups)
¼ cup chopped onion
2 teaspoons instant chicken bouillon granules
1 clove garlic, minced
1 can (16 oz.) red kidney beans or Great
    Northern beans, rinsed and drained
¼ cup green pepper strips (2 x ¼-inch strips)
¼ cup red pepper strips (2 x ¼-inch strips)
1 tablespoon olive oil
1 tablespoon red wine vinegar
2 teaspoons dried parsley flakes
¼ teaspoon dried rosemary leaves, crushed

8 servings

1 Place water in 3-quart saucepan. Bring to boil over high heat. Add potatoes, onion, bouillon and garlic. Return to boil. Cover. Reduce heat to low. Cook for 10 to 12 minutes, or until potatoes are tender-crisp. Drain.

2 Add remaining ingredients. Stir to combine. Return to heat. Cook, uncovered, over medium heat for 2 to 3 minutes, or until hot, stirring occasionally. Cover. Let stand for 5 minutes before serving.

Nutrition Facts	Amount/serving	%DV*	Amount/serving	%DV*
Serving Size ½ cup (128g) Servings per Recipe 8 Calories 147 Calories from Fat 20	Total Fat 2g	3%	Total Carbohydrate 27g	9%
	Saturated Fat <1g	1%	Dietary Fiber 5g	21%
	Cholesterol 0mg	0%	Sugars 3g	
	Sodium 233mg	10%	Protein 6g	

Vitamin A 2% • Vitamin C 35% • Calcium 2% • Iron 15%
*Percent Daily Values (DV) are based on a 2000 calorie diet.

Menu Planning Guide
One serving of this recipe provides:
½ Meat, Poultry & Fish
½ Vegetable

Diet Exchanges:
2 starch

PASTA PIZZA

8 oz. uncooked capellini (angel hair spaghetti)

1 tablespoon plus 1 teaspoon olive oil, divided

1/3 cup chopped green pepper

1/4 cup chopped onion

1 1/4 cups low-fat pasta sauce ◆

1/4 cup sliced black olives (optional)

1/2 cup shredded part-skim or nonfat mozzarella cheese ◆

1/4 teaspoon Italian seasoning

6 servings

1 Prepare capellini as directed on package. Rinse and drain. Set aside. In 6-inch nonstick skillet, combine 1 teaspoon oil, the green pepper and onion. Cook over medium-high heat for 3 to 5 minutes, or until vegetables are tender, stirring frequently. Set aside.

2 Heat remaining 1 tablespoon oil over medium-high heat in 10-inch nonstick skillet. Spread capellini in skillet. Cook for 4 to 6 minutes, or until lightly browned on underside.

3 Turn pasta crust onto plate. Slip crust back into skillet browned-side-up. Reduce heat to medium.

4 Spoon sauce evenly over crust. Top evenly with prepared vegetables and the olives. Sprinkle with cheese and Italian seasoning. Cover. Cook for 4 to 5 minutes, or until cheese is melted. Cut pizza into wedges.

Microwave tip: Omit 1 teaspoon oil. In 2-cup measure, combine green pepper and onion. Microwave at High for 2 to 3 minutes, or until vegetables are tender, stirring once. Continue as directed.

◆ Look for Healthy Choice® products at your favorite supermarket.

Nutrition Facts

Serving Size 1/6 pizza (183g)
Servings per Recipe 6
Calories 221
Calories from Fat 50

Amount/serving	%DV*	Amount/serving	%DV*
Total Fat 6g	9%	Total Carbohydrate 35g	12%
Saturated Fat 2g	8%	Dietary Fiber 2g	8%
Cholesterol 5mg	2%	Sugars 2g	
Sodium 300mg	13%	Protein 9g	

Vitamin A 6% • Vitamin C 25% • Calcium 8% • Iron 15%
*Percent Daily Values (DV) are based on a 2000 calorie diet.

Menu Planning Guide

One serving of this recipe provides:
1 Vegetable
2 Bread, Cereal, Rice & Pasta

Diet Exchanges:
2 starch • 1 vegetable • 1/2 fat

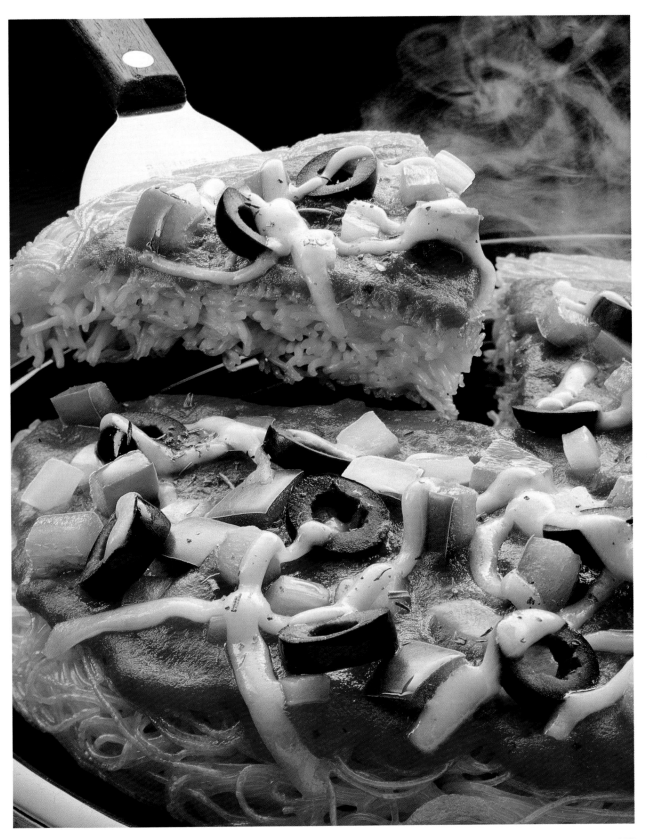

RICE WITH BEANS & JALAPEÑOS

1 cup water

½ cup picante sauce

½ cup sliced green onions

1½ cups uncooked instant white rice

1 can (16 oz.) pinto beans, rinsed and drained

1 tablespoon canned diced jalapeño peppers

½ teaspoon ground cumin (optional)

1 medium tomato, cut into wedges

6 servings

1 Combine water, picante sauce and onions in 2-quart saucepan. Bring to boil over high heat.

2 Stir in rice, beans, peppers and cumin. Cover. Remove from heat. Let stand for 10 minutes.

3 Before serving, fluff rice with fork. Garnish with tomato wedges.

Nutrition Facts	Amount/serving	%DV*	Amount/serving	%DV*
Serving Size approximately 1 cup (237g)	Total Fat <1g	1%	Total Carbohydrate 38g	13%
Servings per Recipe 6	Saturated Fat <1g	1%	Dietary Fiber 7g	28%
Calories 188	Cholesterol <1mg	0%	Sugars 3g	
Calories from Fat 7	Sodium 136mg	6%	Protein 8g	

Vitamin A 4% • Vitamin C 15% • Calcium 6% • Iron 15%

*Percent Daily Values (DV) are based on a 2000 calorie diet.

Menu Planning Guide

One serving of this recipe provides:
1 Bread, Cereal, Rice & Pasta

Diet Exchanges:
2½ starch

TRI-BEAN BAKE

1 medium onion, thinly sliced (1 cup)
1 stalk celery, thinly sliced (½ cup)
1 teaspoon vegetable oil
1 can (16 oz.) pinto beans, rinsed and drained
1 can (15 oz.) butter beans, rinsed and drained
1 can (15 oz.) garbanzo beans, rinsed and
    drained
1 can (8 oz.) tomato sauce
¼ cup frozen apple juice concentrate, defrosted
1 tablespoon light molasses (optional)
½ teaspoon dry mustard

10 servings

1 Heat oven to 375°F. In 10-inch nonstick skillet, combine onion, celery and oil. Cook over medium heat for 5 to 8 minutes, or until vegetables are tender, stirring occasionally.

2 Stir in remaining ingredients. Spoon mixture into 2-quart casserole. Cover. Bake for 25 to 30 minutes, or until hot and bubbly.

Microwave tip: Substitute 1 tablespoon water for oil. In 2-quart casserole, combine onion, celery and water. Cover. Microwave at High for 3 to 6 minutes, or until vegetables are tender, stirring once. Stir in remaining ingredients. Re-cover. Microwave at High for 13 to 15 minutes, or until hot and bubbly, stirring twice.

Nutrition Facts	Amount/serving	%DV*	Amount/serving	%DV*
Serving Size approximately 1 cup (168g) Servings per Recipe 10 Calories 182 Calories from Fat 17	Total Fat 2g	3%	Total Carbohydrate 34g	11%
	Saturated Fat <1g	1%	Dietary Fiber 9g	36%
	Cholesterol 0mg	0%	Sugars 7g	
	Sodium 241mg	10%	Protein 9g	
	Vitamin A 4% • Vitamin C 15% • Calcium 6% • Iron 15%			
	*Percent Daily Values (DV) are based on a 2000 calorie diet.			

Menu Planning Guide
One serving of this recipe provides:
½ Meat, Poultry & Fish

Diet Exchanges:
2½ starch

POLYNESIAN PILAF

1   can (8 oz.) pineapple tidbits in juice, drained
    (reserve juice)
2   cups uncooked instant white rice
6   oz. fresh snow pea pods, trimmed (2 cups)
2   tablespoons reduced-sodium soy sauce
1   tablespoon packed brown sugar
2   teaspoons sliced pimiento, drained
½   teaspoon ground ginger
¼   teaspoon salt

6 servings

1 Combine reserved juice and enough water to equal 1⅔ cups in 2-cup measure. In 2-quart saucepan, combine juice mixture and remaining ingredients, except pineapple. Bring to boil over high heat. Cook for 1½ minutes, stirring occasionally.

2 Remove from heat. Stir in pineapple. Let stand, covered, for 5 to 7 minutes, or until rice is tender and liquid is absorbed. Before serving, fluff rice with fork.

Microwave tip: In 2-quart casserole, combine juice mixture and remaining ingredients, except pineapple. Cover. Microwave at High for 10 to 12 minutes, or until rice is tender and liquid is absorbed. Stir in pineapple. Re-cover. Let stand for 5 minutes. Before serving, fluff rice with fork.

Nutrition Facts	Amount/serving	%DV*	Amount/serving	%DV*
Serving Size approximately 1 cup (249g)	Total Fat <1g	0%	Total Carbohydrate 35g	12%
Servings per Recipe 6	Saturated Fat <1g	0%	Dietary Fiber 2g	8%
Calories 160	Cholesterol 0mg	0%	Sugars 9g	
Calories from Fat 3	Sodium 297mg	12%	Protein 4g	

Vitamin A 2% • Vitamin C 60% • Calcium 4% • Iron 10%

*Percent Daily Values (DV) are based on a 2000 calorie diet.

Menu Planning Guide
One serving of this recipe provides:
½   Vegetable
2   Bread, Cereal, Rice & Pasta

Diet Exchanges:
2 starch • ½ vegetable

CURRIED FRUIT PASTA SALAD

1   pkg. (7 oz.) uncooked elbow macaroni
1   can (20 oz.) pineapple chunks in juice, drained
2   cups seedless red grapes
2   stalks celery, sliced (1 cup)
¼   to ½ cup sliced green onions

Dressing:

¼   cup plain nonfat or low-fat yogurt
2   tablespoons frozen orange juice
      concentrate, defrosted
1   to 1½ teaspoons curry powder
1½ teaspoons lemon juice
½   teaspoon sugar

8 servings

1 Prepare macaroni as directed on package. Rinse with cold water. Drain.

2 Combine pasta, pineapple, grapes, celery and onions in large mixing bowl.

3 Combine dressing ingredients in small mixing bowl. Add to pasta mixture. Toss to coat. Serve on lettuce-lined plates.

Nutrition Facts	Amount/serving	%DV*	Amount/serving	%DV*
Serving Size approximately 1 cup (201g)	Total Fat 1g	2%	Total Carbohydrate 38g	13%
Servings per Recipe 8	Saturated Fat <1g	1%	Dietary Fiber 2g	9%
	Cholesterol <1mg	0%	Sugars 18g	
Calories 171	Sodium 22mg	1%	Protein 5g	
Calories from Fat 9	Vitamin A 2% • Vitamin C 35% • Calcium 4% • Iron 8%			
	*Percent Daily Values (DV) are based on a 2000 calorie diet.			

Menu Planning Guide

One serving of this recipe provides:
1 Fruit
1 Bread, Cereal, Rice & Pasta

Diet Exchanges:

1½ starch • 1 fruit

BLACK BEAN CHILI

4 cans (15 oz. each) black beans, rinsed
   and drained, divided
1 can (14½ oz.) ready-to-serve chicken broth
1 small onion, chopped (½ cup)
1 stalk celery, thinly sliced (½ cup)
⅓ cup chopped green pepper
2 cloves garlic, minced
2 teaspoons olive oil
1 can (14½ oz.) whole tomatoes, undrained
   and cut up

2 teaspoons chili powder
½ teaspoon ground cumin
½ teaspoon dried oregano leaves
¼ teaspoon salt
½ cup chopped seeded tomato
½ cup sliced green onions
2 tablespoons plus 2 teaspoons plain nonfat
   or low-fat yogurt

8 servings

1 Place 3 cups beans and the broth in food processor or blender. Process until smooth. Set aside.

2 Combine onion, celery, pepper, garlic and oil in 3-quart saucepan. Cook over medium heat for 8 to 10 minutes, or until vegetables are tender, stirring frequently. Add processed beans, remaining beans, the canned tomatoes, chili powder, cumin, oregano and salt. Mix well.

3 Bring to boil over high heat, stirring occasionally. Reduce heat to low. Cook for 10 to 15 minutes, or until chili is hot and flavors are blended, stirring occasionally. Garnish each serving with 1 tablespoon each chopped tomato and green onion, and 1 teaspoon yogurt.

Nutrition Facts	Amount/serving	%DV*	Amount/serving	%DV*
Serving Size approximately 1 cup (335g)	Total Fat 3g	4%	Total Carbohydrate 50g	17%
Servings per Recipe 8	Saturated Fat 1g	3%	Dietary Fiber 18g	72%
Calories 290 Calories from Fat 25	Cholesterol <1mg	0%	Sugars 7g	
	Sodium 335mg	14%	Protein 19g	

Vitamin A 15% • Vitamin C 30% • Calcium 10% • Iron 25%
*Percent Daily Values (DV) are based on a 2000 calorie diet.

Menu Planning Guide
One serving of this recipe provides:
1 Meat, Poultry & Fish
1 Vegetable

Diet Exchanges:
3 starch • 1 vegetable

PASTA PRIMAVERA

12 oz. uncooked mini lasagna noodles

2 cups fresh broccoli flowerets

6 oz. fresh mushrooms, sliced (2 cups)

1 medium yellow squash, cut into 1½ x ¼-inch strips (1 cup)

1 medium zucchini squash, cut into 1½ x ¼-inch strips (1 cup)

1 medium carrot, sliced (½ cup)

2½ cups water, divided

1 cup nonfat dry milk powder

3 tablespoons all-purpose flour

2 large cloves garlic, minced

2 teaspoons dried oregano leaves

1 teaspoon dried basil leaves

½ to 1 teaspoon fennel seed, crushed

½ teaspoon salt

½ teaspoon pepper

1 cup shredded nonfat or part-skim mozzarella cheese ◆

1 tablespoon snipped fresh parsley
Shredded fresh Parmesan cheese (optional)

10 servings

1 Prepare noodles as directed on package. Rinse. Let stand in warm water. In 6-quart Dutch oven or stockpot, combine broccoli, mushrooms, squashes, carrot and ½ cup water. Cover. Cook over high heat for 5 to 7 minutes, or until vegetables are tender-crisp, stirring occasionally. Drain. Set aside.

2 Combine dry milk, flour, garlic, oregano, basil, fennel, salt and pepper in 2-quart saucepan. Blend in remaining 2 cups water. Cook over medium-low heat for 20 to 25 minutes, or until sauce thickens and bubbles, stirring frequently.

3 Remove from heat. Add mozzarella cheese. Stir until melted. In large mixing bowl or serving bowl, combine sauce, noodles and vegetables. Toss to combine. Garnish with parsley and Parmesan cheese.

Microwave tip: In 8-cup measure, combine dry milk, flour, garlic, oregano, basil, fennel, salt and pepper. Blend in remaining 2 cups water. Microwave at High for 5 to 8 minutes, or until sauce thickens and bubbles, stirring with whisk after every minute. Continue as directed.

◆ Look for Healthy Choice® products at your favorite supermarket.

Nutrition Facts	Amount/serving	%DV*	Amount/serving	%DV*
Serving Size approximately 1 cup (243g)	Total Fat 1g	2%	Total Carbohydrate 40g	13%
Servings per Recipe 10	Saturated Fat <1g	0%	Dietary Fiber 3g	12%
Calories 218	Cholesterol 3mg	1%	Sugars 7g	
Calories from Fat 9	Sodium 235mg	10%	Protein 13g	

Vitamin A 50% • Vitamin C 30% • Calcium 10% • Iron 15%
*Percent Daily Values (DV) are based on a 2000 calorie diet.

Menu Planning Guide
One serving of this recipe provides:
1 Milk, Yogurt & Cheese
1 Vegetable
2 Bread, Cereal, Rice & Pasta

Diet Exchanges:
½ lean meat • 2 starch • 1 vegetable

NO-GUILT REFRIED BEANS

1 can (16 oz.) pinto beans, rinsed and drained
¼ cup thick and chunky salsa
2 tablespoons finely chopped onion
⅛ teaspoon garlic powder
1 tablespoon margarine

4 servings

1 Combine beans, salsa, onion and garlic powder in 2-quart saucepan. Bring mixture to boil over medium-high heat, stirring occasionally. Reduce heat to medium-low. Simmer for 7 to 10 minutes, or until onion is translucent, stirring occasionally.

2 Add margarine. Stir until melted. In food processor or blender, process mixture until smooth. Serve as a taco ingredient or chip and vegetable dip.

Nutrition Facts	Amount/serving	%DV*	Amount/serving	%DV*	Menu Planning Guide
Serving Size approximately ¼ cup (121g)	Total Fat 3g	5%	Total Carbohydrate 26g	9%	One serving of this recipe provides: ½ Meat, Poultry & Fish
	Saturated Fat <1g	4%	Dietary Fiber 9g	36%	
Servings per Recipe 4	Cholesterol 0mg	0%	Sugars 3g		
	Sodium 94mg	4%	Protein 8g		
Calories 165 Calories from Fat 31	Vitamin A 8% • Vitamin C 15% • Calcium 6% • Iron 15%				Diet Exchanges: 2 starch
	*Percent Daily Values (DV) are based on a 2000 calorie diet.				

PASTA WITH FRESH TOMATO SAUCE

1 tablespoon margarine

1 medium onion, chopped (1 cup)

3 medium tomatoes, peeled and cut into 1-inch cubes (3 cups)

1 can (6 oz.) tomato paste

½ cup dry red wine

¼ cup snipped fresh Italian parsley leaves

3 anchovy fillets, finely chopped

1 clove garlic, minced

1 teaspoon instant beef bouillon granules

½ teaspoon sugar

6 cups hot cooked pasta

6 servings

1 Melt margarine over medium heat in 3-quart saucepan. Add onion. Cook for 5 to 7 minutes, or until onion is tender, stirring occasionally.

2 Stir in remaining ingredients, except pasta. Bring to boil over high heat. Reduce heat to low. Cook for 20 to 25 minutes, or until tomatoes are tender and sauce is slightly thickened, stirring occasionally. Serve over pasta.

Nutrition Facts	Amount/serving	%DV*	Amount/serving	%DV*
Serving Size approximately 1½ cups (231g) Servings per Recipe 6 Calories 249 Calories from Fat 36	Total Fat 4g	6%	Total Carbohydrate 45g	15%
	Saturated Fat <1g	3%	Dietary Fiber 4g	16%
	Cholesterol 48mg	16%	Sugars 4g	
	Sodium 338mg	14%	Protein 10g	
	Vitamin A 25% • Vitamin C 40% • Calcium 4% • Iron 15%			
	*Percent Daily Values (DV) are based on a 2000 calorie diet.			

Menu Planning Guide
One serving of this recipe provides:
2 Vegetable
2 Bread, Cereal, Rice & Pasta

Diet Exchanges:
2 starch • 2 vegetable • ½ fat

RICE & VEGETABLE CROQUETTES

  1   cup uncooked instant white rice
 ⅓   cup finely chopped red pepper
 ¼   cup shredded carrot
 ¼   cup sliced green onions
  2   egg whites

  1   tablespoon all-purpose flour
 ¼   teaspoon dried thyme leaves
 ¼   teaspoon salt

4 servings

1 Prepare rice as directed on package. Set aside. Spray 10-inch nonstick skillet with nonstick vegetable cooking spray. Add pepper, carrot and onions. Cook over medium heat for 5 to 8 minutes, or until vegetables are tender-crisp, stirring frequently. (If vegetables begin to stick, move them to one side and spray skillet with nonstick vegetable cooking spray.) Remove from heat. Cool slightly. Add vegetable mixture, egg whites, flour, thyme and salt to rice.

2 Wipe skillet with paper towel. Spray with nonstick vegetable cooking spray. Heat skillet over medium heat. Drop ⅓ cup rice mixture into skillet, flattening with back of spatula to form 3½-inch patty. Repeat with remaining rice mixture. Cook for 4 to 7 minutes, or until light golden brown, turning patties over once.

Nutrition Facts	Amount/serving	%DV*	Amount/serving	%DV*
Serving Size 1 patty (126g) Servings per Recipe 4 Calories 105 Calories from Fat 2	Total Fat <1g	0%	Total Carbohydrate 21g	7%
	Saturated Fat 0g	0%	Dietary Fiber 1g	4%
	Cholesterol 0mg	0%	Sugars 1g	
	Sodium 167mg	7%	Protein 4g	

Vitamin A 50% • Vitamin C 35% • Calcium 2% • Iron 6%
*Percent Daily Values (DV) are based on a 2000 calorie diet.

Menu Planning Guide
One serving of this recipe provides:
½ Vegetable
 1 Bread, Cereal, Rice & Pasta

Diet Exchanges:
1 starch • ½ vegetable

PASTA WITH ONION SAUCE

6 oz. uncooked linguine or fettucini

1 medium red onion, thinly sliced
   and separated into rings

1 medium carrot, thinly sliced (1/2 cup)

1/4 cup chopped red pepper

1/4 cup water

1 cup skim milk

2 tablespoons all-purpose flour

2 tablespoons dry white wine

1 teaspoon instant chicken bouillon granules

1/4 teaspoon salt

1/8 teaspoon black pepper

2 tablespoons grated Parmesan cheese

8 servings

1 Prepare linguine as directed on package. Rinse. Let stand in warm water. Set aside. In 2-quart saucepan, combine onion, carrot, red pepper and water. Cook over medium-high heat for 6 to 7 minutes, or until vegetables are tender, stirring occasionally.

2 Reduce heat to low. In 2-cup measure, combine remaining ingredients, except Parmesan cheese. Add to onion mixture. Cook for 6 to 10 minutes, or until sauce thickens and bubbles, stirring frequently. Remove from heat. Stir in Parmesan cheese.

3 Drain linguine. In large mixing bowl or serving bowl, combine linguine and sauce. Toss to combine. Serve hot.

Nutrition Facts	Amount/serving	%DV*	Amount/serving	%DV*
Serving Size 1/2 cup (125g)	Total Fat 1g	2%	Total Carbohydrate 22g	7%
Servings per Recipe 8	Saturated Fat <1g	2%	Dietary Fiber 2g	8%
Calories 118	Cholesterol 2mg	0%	Sugars 4g	
Calories from Fat 9	Sodium 231mg	10%	Protein 5g	

Vitamin A 45% • Vitamin C 15% • Calcium 6% • Iron 6%
*Percent Daily Values (DV) are based on a 2000 calorie diet.

Menu Planning Guide

One serving of this recipe provides:

1/2 Vegetable
1 Bread, Cereal, Rice & Pasta

Diet Exchanges:

1 starch • 1/2 vegetable

EGGS & CHEESE

TOMATO CHEESE PIE

Crust:

½ cup all-purpose flour

½ cup whole wheat flour

1 tablespoon yellow cornmeal

¼ teaspoon salt (optional)

3 tablespoons margarine, cut up

3 to 4 tablespoons ice water

Filling:

1 cup nonfat or light ricotta cheese

½ cup nonfat or low-fat cottage cheese

½ cup shredded nonfat Cheddar cheese ◆

½ cup frozen cholesterol-free egg product ◆,
defrosted, or 2 eggs

2 tablespoons all-purpose flour

½ teaspoon dried oregano leaves

¼ teaspoon garlic powder

1 medium tomato, thinly sliced

1 tablespoon grated Parmesan cheese (optional)

1 tablespoon snipped fresh parsley

¼ teaspoon dried oregano leaves

6 servings

1 Heat oven to 375°F. In medium mixing bowl, combine flours, cornmeal and salt. Cut in margarine until mixture resembles coarse crumbs. Sprinkle with water, 1 tablespoon at a time, mixing with fork until particles are moistened and cling together.

2 Form dough into ball. Place between 2 sheets of wax paper. Roll out dough into 12-inch circle. Remove top sheet of wax paper. Turn circle onto 9-inch pie plate; remove second sheet of wax paper. Trim and flute edge. Set aside.

3 Combine filling ingredients in medium mixing bowl. Spoon into prepared crust. Bake for 30 minutes. Top with tomato slices. Sprinkle remaining ingredients evenly over tomato.

4 Bake for additional 10 to 15 minutes, or until knife inserted in center of pie comes out clean. Let stand for 10 minutes before serving.

Nutrition Facts	Amount/serving	%DV*	Amount/serving	%DV*
Serving Size ⅙ pie (129g)	Total Fat 10g	15%	Total Carbohydrate 23g	8%
Servings per Recipe 6	Saturated Fat 2g	11%	Dietary Fiber 2g	8%
Calories 231	Cholesterol 12mg	4%	Sugars 2g	
Calories from Fat 87	Sodium 350mg	15%	Protein 13g	

Vitamin A 10% • Vitamin C 8% • Calcium 30% • Iron 10%

*Percent Daily Values (DV) are based on a 2000 calorie diet.

Menu Planning Guide

One serving of this recipe provides:

½ Milk, Yogurt & Cheese
1 Bread, Cereal, Rice & Pasta

Diet Exchanges:

1 lean meat • 1½ starch • 1 fat

THREE-CHEESE STUFFED MANICOTTI

8 uncooked manicotti shells

1¾ cups low-fat pasta sauce ◆, divided

1 pkg. (9 oz.) frozen chopped spinach, defrosted and well drained

1 cup low-fat or nonfat ricotta cheese

2 egg whites, slightly beaten

1 tablespoon shredded fresh Parmesan cheese

¼ teaspoon garlic powder

½ cup shredded part-skim or nonfat mozzarella cheese ◆

4 servings

1 Heat oven to 400°F. Prepare manicotti shells as directed on package. Rinse. Let stand in warm water.

2 Spread ¾ cup sauce in 12 x 8-inch baking dish. Set aside.

3 Combine spinach, ricotta cheese, egg whites, Parmesan cheese and garlic powder in medium mixing bowl. Drain shells. Stuff each shell with heaping ¼ cup spinach mixture. Arrange stuffed shells over sauce in baking dish.

4 Spoon remaining 1 cup sauce over shells. Cover with foil. Bake for 15 to 20 minutes, or until sauce bubbles. Sprinkle with mozzarella. Bake, uncovered, for 5 to 7 minutes, or until cheese is melted.

◆ Look for Healthy Choice® products at your favorite supermarket.

Nutrition Facts	Amount/serving	%DV*	Amount/serving	%DV*
Serving Size 2 shells (297g)	Total Fat 8g	12%	Total Carbohydrate 26g	9%
Servings per Recipe 4	Saturated Fat 4g	19%	Dietary Fiber 2g	10%
Calories 239	Cholesterol 29mg	10%	Sugars 1g	
Calories from Fat 70	Sodium 555mg	23%	Protein 18g	

Vitamin A 60% • Vitamin C 50% • Calcium 45% • Iron 20%

*Percent Daily Values (DV) are based on a 2000 calorie diet.

Menu Planning Guide
One serving of this recipe provides:

1 Milk, Yogurt & Cheese
2 Vegetable
1 Bread, Cereal, Rice & Pasta

Diet Exchanges:
1½ lean meat • 1 starch • 2 vegetable

ITALIAN OMELET

2 teaspoons sliced black olives, drained

1/2 teaspoon diced pimiento, drained

1/2 cup low-fat or nonfat ricotta cheese

1 teaspoon snipped fresh basil leaves

1/4 to 1/2 teaspoon garlic powder

1/8 teaspoon pepper

1 cup frozen cholesterol-free egg product ◆, defrosted; or 4 eggs, beaten

1/4 cup nonfat pasta sauce ◆

Shredded fresh Parmesan cheese (optional)

2 servings

1 Blot olives and pimiento with paper towel to remove excess moisture. In small mixing bowl, combine olives, pimiento, ricotta cheese, basil, garlic powder and pepper. Set aside.

2 Spray 10-inch nonstick skillet with nonstick vegetable cooking spray. Heat skillet over medium heat. Pour egg product into skillet. Lift edges of cooked egg product with spatula and tilt skillet to permit uncooked egg product to run to bottom of skillet. Cook for 1½ to 2½ minutes, or until omelet is still moist, but nearly set.

3 Spread cheese mixture evenly over bottom half of omelet. Loosen sides of omelet with spatula. Fold top half over bottom half. Cook for 2 to 3 minutes, or until filling is hot and omelet is set. Slide omelet onto serving plate. In 1-quart saucepan, heat pasta sauce over medium heat for 1 to 2 minutes, or until hot, stirring occasionally. Spoon sauce over omelet. Garnish with Parmesan cheese.

Microwave tip: Place pasta sauce in 1-cup measure. Cover with plastic wrap. Microwave at High for 30 to 45 seconds, or until hot. Continue as directed.

◆ Look for Healthy Choice® products at your favorite supermarket.

Nutrition Facts

Serving Size
1/2 omelet (192g)
Servings
per Recipe 2

Calories 145
Calories
from Fat 35

Amount/serving	%DV*	Amount/serving	%DV*
Total Fat 4g	6%	Total Carbohydrate 8g	3%
Saturated Fat 2g	9%	Dietary Fiber <1g	1%
Cholesterol 17mg	6%	Sugars <1g	
Sodium 332mg	14%	Protein 16g	

Vitamin A 25% • Vitamin C 10% • Calcium 25% • Iron 10%

*Percent Daily Values (DV) are based on a 2000 calorie diet.

Menu Planning Guide

One serving of this recipe provides:

1/2 Milk, Yogurt & Cheese
1/2 Meat, Poultry & Fish
1/2 Vegetable

Diet Exchanges:

2 lean meat • 1/2 vegetable

214

EGG FOO YOUNG

¼ cup finely chopped green pepper
2 tablespoons finely chopped onion
2 small cloves garlic, minced
1 teaspoon vegetable oil
1 cup fresh bean sprouts
1 cup frozen cholesterol-free egg product ◆,
   defrosted, or 4 eggs
1 tablespoon plus 1 teaspoon cornstarch
¼ teaspoon salt

Sauce:

2 teaspoons cornstarch
½ teaspoon sugar
½ teaspoon instant beef bouillon granules
2 teaspoons reduced-sodium soy sauce
1 teaspoon dry white wine
½ cup hot water

4 servings

1 Spray 10-inch nonstick skillet with nonstick vegetable cooking spray. Add pepper, onion, garlic and oil. Cook over medium heat for 4½ to 7 minutes, or until vegetables are tender, stirring occasionally. Remove from heat. Cool slightly. In small mixing bowl, combine vegetable mixture, sprouts, egg product, 1 tablespoon plus 1 teaspoon cornstarch and salt. Set aside.

2 Wipe skillet with paper towel. Spray with nonstick vegetable cooking spray. Heat skillet over high heat. Using ⅓-cup measure, pour mixture into skillet to form 4 patties. Use spatula to keep patties from running together. Cook for 1½ to 2 minutes, or until egg is set and brown, turning patties over once. (For best results, let each patty set up slightly before adding more mixture.) Remove from heat. Cover to keep warm. Set aside.

3 Combine sauce ingredients in 1-quart saucepan. Cook over low heat for 3½ to 9 minutes, or until sauce is thickened and translucent, stirring constantly. Spoon over patties.

◆ Look for Healthy Choice® products at your favorite supermarket.

Nutrition Facts	Amount/serving	%DV*	Amount/serving	%DV*
Serving Size 1 patty (137g)	Total Fat 2g	3%	Total Carbohydrate 10g	3%
Servings per Recipe 4	Saturated Fat <1g	1%	Dietary Fiber 1g	4%
Calories 81	Cholesterol 0mg	0%	Sugars 4g	
Calories from Fat 15	Sodium 343mg	14%	Protein 7g	

Vitamin A 10% • Vitamin C 20% • Calcium 2% • Iron 8%
*Percent Daily Values (DV) are based on a 2000 calorie diet.

Menu Planning Guide
One serving of this recipe provides:
1 Vegetable

Diet Exchanges:
½ lean meat • 1 vegetable

SPAETZLE

8½ cups water, divided
1½ cups all-purpose flour
½ cup frozen cholesterol-free egg product ◆,
    defrosted, or 2 eggs
1 teaspoon salt, divided

4 cups ice water
1 tablespoon margarine
1 clove garlic, minced
1 tablespoon snipped fresh parsley

8 servings

1 Combine ½ cup water, the flour, egg product and ½ teaspoon salt in medium mixing bowl. Stir with wooden spoon until well blended. Set aside.

2 Combine remaining 8 cups water and ½ teaspoon salt in 4-quart saucepan. Bring to boil over medium-high heat. Using a spatula, scrape small amount of batter through back side of coarse grater over boiling water. (Batter should drop in small pieces.) When spaetzle floats to surface of water, remove with slotted spoon and place in ice water. Repeat with remaining batter. Drain water from spaetzle. Set aside.

3 Melt margarine in 10-inch nonstick skillet over medium heat. Add garlic and spaetzle. Cook for 7 to 10 minutes, or until spaetzle is hot and just begins to brown, stirring occasionally. Stir in parsley. Serve hot.

◆ Look for Healthy Choice® products at your favorite supermarket.

Nutrition Facts	Amount/serving	%DV*	Amount/serving	%DV*	Menu Planning Guide
Serving Size approximately ½ cup (55g)	Total Fat 2g	3%	Total Carbohydrate 18g	6%	One serving of this recipe provides:
	Saturated Fat <1g	2%	Dietary Fiber <1g	3%	1 Bread, Cereal, Rice & Pasta
Servings per Recipe 8	Cholesterol 0mg	0%	Sugars 1g		
Calories 106	Sodium 174mg	7%	Protein 4g		
Calories from Fat 16	Vitamin A 4% • Vitamin C 2% • Calcium 2% • Iron 8%				Diet Exchanges:
	*Percent Daily Values (DV) are based on a 2000 calorie diet.				1 starch

PEACH BLINTZES

Blintzes:

  1 *cup skim milk*

  ¾ *cup all-purpose flour*

  ¼ *cup frozen cholesterol-free egg product* ◆,
      defrosted; or 1 egg, beaten

  2 *teaspoons sugar*

     Dash salt

Filling:

1½ *cups nonfat or low-fat cottage cheese, drained*

  ¼ *cup finely chopped peeled fresh peach*

  2 *tablespoons sugar*

  1 *tablespoon orange marmalade*

  ¼ *teaspoon vanilla*

Sauce:

  ½ *cup vanilla nonfat or low-fat yogurt*

  1 *tablespoon honey*

  2 *fresh peaches, peeled, pitted and thinly sliced*

5 servings

Tip: Drained canned peaches in juice or frozen peaches can be substituted for fresh peaches.

1 Combine blintz ingredients in medium mixing bowl. Beat with whisk until batter is smooth. Spray 7-inch nonstick skillet with nonstick vegetable cooking spray. Heat skillet over medium-high heat.

2 Add 3 scant tablespoons batter to skillet, tilting skillet to coat bottom. Cook for 30 seconds to 1 minute, or until blintz is lightly browned on both sides, turning blintz over after half the time. Repeat with remaining batter, stacking blintzes between sheets of wax paper. (Spray skillet with nonstick vegetable cooking spray between blintzes.) Set aside.

3 Combine filling ingredients in small mixing bowl. Set aside. In small bowl, combine sauce ingredients. Set aside. Spoon 3 scant tablespoons filling down center of each blintz. Roll up. Place blintzes on serving plates. Arrange peach slices and spoon sauce evenly over blintzes.

Tip: If desired, arrange rolled blintzes in 13 x 9-inch baking pan. Bake in 350°F oven for 10 to 15 minutes, or until hot. Arrange peach slices and spoon sauce evenly over hot blintzes.

◆ Look for Healthy Choice® products at your favorite supermarket.

Nutrition Facts	Amount/serving	%DV*	Amount/serving	%DV*
Serving Size 2 blintzes (220g) Servings per Recipe 5 Calories 209 Calories from Fat 4	Total Fat 1g	1%	Total Carbohydrate 38g	13%
	Saturated Fat 0g	0%	Dietary Fiber 2g	6%
	Cholesterol 4mg	1%	Sugars 23g	
	Sodium 309mg	13%	Protein 14g	

Vitamin A 8% • Vitamin C 6% • Calcium 15% • Iron 6%

*Percent Daily Values (DV) are based on a 2000 calorie diet.

Menu Planning Guide
One serving of this recipe provides:
½ Milk, Yogurt & Cheese
½ Fruit
1 Bread, Cereal, Rice & Pasta

Diet Exchanges:
1 lean meat • ½ skim milk • 1½ starch • ½ fruit

BAKING & DESSERTS

BLACKBERRY PAVLOVAS*

3 egg whites, room temperature
¼ teaspoon cream of tartar
¼ teaspoon vanilla
¾ cup sugar
1 pkg. (3.4 oz.) instant vanilla or lemon
    pudding and pie filling
1½ cups skim milk
1 can (16½ oz.) blackberries, drained

6 servings

*Pavlova, a meringue-based dessert from Australia,
was named for the famous Russian ballerina,
Anna Pavlova.*

1 Heat oven to 225°F. Line large baking sheet with parchment paper. Trace six 3½-inch circles on paper. Set aside.

2 Combine egg whites, cream of tartar and vanilla in large mixing bowl. Beat at high speed of electric mixer until soft peaks begin to form. Add sugar, 1 tablespoon at a time, while beating at high speed. Beat until mixture is thick and glossy.

3 Spread about ½ cup meringue mixture over each circle on prepared baking sheet, mounding slightly around edges. Bake for 2 hours. Turn oven off. (Do not open door.) Let meringues stand in oven for 1 hour. Remove from oven and cool to room temperature. Set aside.

4 Combine pudding mix and milk in 4-cup measure. Stir well with whisk to combine. Let stand for 5 minutes, or until thickened.

5 Peel paper carefully from meringues. Place meringues on serving platter. Spoon ¼ cup pudding into each meringue. Top evenly with blackberries.

Nutrition Facts	Amount/serving	%DV*	Amount/serving	%DV*	Menu Planning Guide
Serving Size 1 meringue (187g)	Total Fat <1g	1%	Total Carbohydrate 52g	17%	One serving of this recipe provides: 1 Fruit
Servings per Recipe 6	Saturated Fat <1g	1%	Dietary Fiber 3g	14%	
Calories 222	Cholesterol 1mg	0%	Sugars 33g		
Calories from Fat 5	Sodium 291mg	12%	Protein 4g		

Vitamin A 4% • Vitamin C 25% • Calcium 10% • Iron 2%
*Percent Daily Values (DV) are based on a 2000 calorie diet.

Diet Exchanges:
3 starch • 1 fruit

APPLE & APRICOT POACHED PEARS

  2 *tablespoons sugar*
  1 *tablespoon plus 1 teaspoon cornstarch*
1½ *cups unsweetened apple juice*
  1 *teaspoon vanilla*
 ⅓ *cup dried apricots, chopped*

  2 *fresh Bartlett pears, cored and cut in half*
     lengthwise
     Chopped crystallized ginger (optional)

4 servings

1 Combine sugar and cornstarch in 2-quart saucepan. Blend in juice and vanilla. Stir in apricots. Cook over medium heat for 4 to 6 minutes, or until mixture is slightly thickened and transluscent and begins to bubble, stirring frequently.

2 Reduce heat to medium-low. Add pear halves. Cook for 10 to 18 minutes, or until pears are tender. Using slotted spoon, remove pears from poaching liquid. Serve warm or chilled with poaching liquid. Lightly sprinkle each serving with ginger.

Nutrition Facts	Amount/serving	%DV*	Amount/serving	%DV*	**Menu Planning Guide**
Serving Size ½ pear (196g)	Total Fat <1g	1%	Total Carbohydrate 41g	14%	One serving of this recipe provides: 2 Fruit
Servings per Recipe 4	Saturated Fat <1g	0%	Dietary Fiber 2g	8%	
Calories 162	Cholesterol 0mg	0%	Sugars 28g		
Calories from Fat 0	Sodium 5mg	0%	Protein <1g		

Vitamin A 15% • Vitamin C 8% • Calcium 2% • Iron 6%

*Percent Daily Values (DV) are based on a 2000 calorie diet.

Diet Exchanges:
1 starch • 2 fruit

HONEY-GLAZED CRANBERRY CORNMEAL MUFFINS

1 cup all-purpose flour

1 cup yellow cornmeal

2 teaspoons baking powder

¼ teaspoon ground allspice

⅛ teaspoon salt

¾ cup low-fat or nonfat buttermilk

¼ cup frozen cholesterol-free egg product ◆,
  defrosted; or 1 egg, beaten

¼ cup honey

2 tablespoons vegetable oil

1 teaspoon grated orange peel

½ cup chopped fresh or frozen cranberries*

Glaze:

¼ cup powdered sugar

1 tablespoon honey

1 tablespoon water

1 dozen muffins

If desired, substitute dried cranberries or raisins for fresh cranberries.

1 Heat oven to 400°F. Spray 12 muffin cups with nonstick vegetable cooking spray, or line cups with paper liners. Set aside.

2 Combine flour, cornmeal, baking powder, allspice and salt in large mixing bowl. Add buttermilk, egg product, honey, oil and peel. Stir just until dry ingredients are moistened. Fold in cranberries.

3 Spoon batter evenly into prepared muffin cups. Bake for 13 to 15 minutes, or until lightly browned. Loosen muffins from rim of pan. Place on cooling rack.

4 Combine glaze ingredients in small mixing bowl. Drizzle over warm muffins. Serve warm.

◆ Look for Healthy Choice® products at your favorite supermarket.

Nutrition Facts	Amount/serving	%DV*	Amount/serving	%DV*	Menu Planning Guide
Serving Size 1 muffin (60g)	Total Fat 3g	5%	Total Carbohydrate 28g	9%	One serving of this recipe provides: 1 Bread, Cereal, Rice & Pasta
Servings per Recipe 12	Saturated Fat <1g	2%	Dietary Fiber 1g	6%	
Calories 151	Cholesterol <1mg	0%	Sugars 11g		
Calories from Fat 30	Sodium 122mg	5%	Protein 3g		
	Vitamin A 2% • Vitamin C 2% • Calcium 6% • Iron 6%				
	*Percent Daily Values (DV) are based on a 2000 calorie diet.				

Diet Exchanges:
2 starch

228

PINEAPPLE CARROT CAKE

Cake:

½ cup all-purpose flour

½ cup whole wheat flour

½ cup packed brown sugar

1 teaspoon pumpkin pie spice

1 teaspoon baking powder

½ teaspoon baking soda

1 can (8 oz.) crushed pineapple in juice, drained
  (reserve 3 tablespoons juice for topping)

½ cup frozen cholesterol-free egg product ◆,
  defrosted, or 2 eggs

¼ cup vegetable oil

1 cup shredded carrots

½ cup raisins (optional)

Topping:

4 oz. light or nonfat cream cheese ◆, softened

⅓ cup powdered sugar

¼ teaspoon pumpkin pie spice

8 servings

1 Heat oven to 350°F. Spray 9-inch round cake pan with nonstick vegetable cooking spray. Dust lightly with all-purpose flour. Set aside.

2 Combine all cake ingredients except carrots and raisins in large mixing bowl. Beat at low speed of electric mixer just until combined. Beat at high speed for 2 minutes, scraping bowl frequently. Fold in carrots and raisins. Pour batter into prepared pan. Bake for 20 to 25 minutes, or until wooden pick inserted in center comes out clean.

3 Remove cake from pan. Place on serving plate. In small mixing bowl, combine all topping ingredients and reserved juice. Beat at medium speed of electric mixer until smooth. Spread topping on cooled cake. Sprinkle with additional shredded carrot, if desired.

Microwave tip: Microwave prepared topping at High for 30 to 45 seconds, or until warm, stirring once. Spoon warm topping over wedges of warm cake.

◆ Look for Healthy Choice® products at your favorite supermarket.

Nutrition Facts	Amount/serving	%DV*	Amount/serving	%DV*
Serving Size ⅛ cake (103g)	Total Fat 8g	13%	Total Carbohydrate 33g	11%
Servings per Recipe 8	Saturated Fat 1g	6%	Dietary Fiber 2g	7%
Calories 230	Cholesterol 5mg	1%	Sugars 21g	
Calories from Fat 70	Sodium 220mg	9%	Protein 5g	

Vitamin A 45% • Vitamin C 6% • Calcium 6% • Iron 8%

*Percent Daily Values (DV) are based on a 2000 calorie diet.

Menu Planning Guide
One serving of this recipe provides:
1 Bread, Cereal, Rice & Pasta

Diet Exchanges:
2 starch • 1 fat

WHOLE WHEAT ONION BREAD

1 small onion, finely chopped (¹/₂ cup)
¹/₂ cup thinly sliced green onions
1 cup all-purpose flour
1 cup whole wheat flour
¹/₄ cup sugar
1¹/₂ teaspoons baking soda
¹/₂ teaspoon onion powder
¹/₂ teaspoon dried marjoram leaves
¹/₄ teaspoon salt
1 cup nonfat or low-fat buttermilk
¹/₄ cup frozen cholesterol-free egg product ◆
    defrosted, or 1 egg
2 tablespoons vegetable oil

¹/₂ cup flaked bran cereal, crushed
2 tablespoons snipped fresh chives (optional)

16 servings

1 Heat oven to 375°F. Spray 8¹/₂ x 4¹/₂-inch loaf pan with nonstick vegetable cooking spray. Dust lightly with all-purpose flour. Set aside.

2 Spray 6-inch nonstick skillet with nonstick vegetable cooking spray. Place onions in skillet. Cook over medium heat for 3 to 5 minutes, or until translucent, stirring frequently. Remove from heat. Set aside.

3 Combine flours, sugar, baking soda, onion powder, marjoram and salt in large mixing bowl. Set aside. In small mixing bowl, combine buttermilk, egg product and oil. Stir in onions. Add onion mixture to flour mixture.

4 Beat at medium speed of electric mixer for 1 minute, scraping bowl frequently. Pour batter into prepared pan. Top evenly with cereal and chives.

5 Bake for 45 minutes to 1 hour, or until wooden pick inserted in center comes out clean. Let stand for 10 minutes; remove from pan. Cool completely on wire rack before slicing.

◆ Look for Healthy Choice® products at your favorite supermarket.

Nutrition Facts	Amount/serving	%DV*	Amount/serving	%DV*
Serving Size 1 slice (51g)	Total Fat 3g	4%	Total Carbohydrate 17g	6%
Servings per Recipe 16	Saturated Fat <1g	2%	Dietary Fiber 2g	6%
Calories 101	Cholesterol <1mg	0%	Sugars 5g	
Calories from Fat 22	Sodium 145mg	6%	Protein 3g	

Vitamin A 2% • Vitamin C 2% • Calcium 2% • Iron 8%
*Percent Daily Values (DV) are based on a 2000 calorie diet.

Menu Planning Guide
One serving of this recipe provides:
1 Bread, Cereal, Rice & Pasta

Diet Exchanges:
1 starch

TROPICAL FRUIT COMBO

2 *tablespoons sugar*
1 *tablespoon hot water*
1 *tablespoon fresh lime juice*
2 *cups sliced strawberries, divided*
1 *fresh pineapple*
1 *orange, peeled and sectioned*
1 *kiwifruit, peeled and sliced*
1 *tablespoon plus 1 teaspoon flaked coconut*

4 servings

1 Combine sugar, water and juice in 1-cup measure. Stir until sugar is dissolved. In blender, combine 1 cup strawberries and the sugar mixture. Blend until smooth. Strain mixture through fine-mesh sieve. Discard seeds and pulp. Set sauce aside.

2 Cut pineapple lengthwise into quarters, leaving leaves attached. Remove strip of core from each quarter. Cut fruit from each quarter. Cut pineapple fruit into bite-size pieces.

3 Place pineapple shells on individual serving plates. Arrange pineapple fruit, remaining 1 cup strawberries, the orange sections and kiwifruit slices evenly in each shell. Spoon strawberry sauce and sprinkle coconut evenly over each serving.

Microwave tip: If necessary, microwave sugar mixture at High for 15 to 30 seconds, or until sugar is dissolved, stirring once. Continue as directed.

Nutrition Facts	Amount/serving	%DV*	Amount/serving	%DV*
Serving Size ¼ pineapple (226g)	Total Fat 2g	2%	Total Carbohydrate 31g	10%
Servings per Recipe 4	Saturated Fat <1g	4%	Dietary Fiber 3g	16%
Calories 130	Cholesterol 0mg	0%	Sugars 27g	
Calories from Fat 13	Sodium 3mg	0%	Protein 1g	

Vitamin A 2% • Vitamin C 120% • Calcium 4% • Iron 4%
*Percent Daily Values (DV) are based on a 2000 calorie diet.

Menu Planning Guide
One serving of this recipe provides:
2 Fruit

Diet Exchanges:
2 fruit

FUDGY CHEESECAKE WITH CHERRY SAUCE

2 tablespoons chocolate wafer crumbs (3 wafers)
1 pkg. (8 oz.) low-fat cream cheese, softened
¾ cup plus 2 tablespoons sugar, divided
⅓ cup unsweetened cocoa
1 cup vanilla-flavored nonfat or low-fat yogurt
¼ cup frozen cholesterol-free egg product ◆, defrosted, or 1 egg
1 egg white (2 tablespoons)

2 tablespoons all-purpose flour
1 can (16 oz.) water-packed tart pie cherries, drained (reserve ½ cup liquid)
1 tablespoon plus 1 teaspoon cornstarch

10 servings

1 Heat oven to 325°F. Spray 8-inch springform pan with nonstick vegetable cooking spray. Sprinkle evenly with crumbs. Set aside.

2 Combine cream cheese, ½ cup sugar and the cocoa in medium mixing bowl. Beat at medium speed of electric mixer until creamy. Add yogurt, egg product, egg white and flour. Beat at medium speed until mixture is smooth. Pour into prepared pan. Bake for 40 to 45 minutes, or until set. Cool slightly. Chill at least 2 hours.

3 Combine reserved liquid, remaining 6 tablespoons sugar and the cornstarch in 1-quart saucepan. Cook over medium heat for 2 to 4 minutes, or until mixture is thickened and translucent, stirring constantly. Fold in cherries. Serve sauce warm or chilled with cheesecake.

Microwave tip: In 4-cup measure, combine reserved liquid, remaining 6 tablespoons sugar and the cornstarch. Microwave at High for 2 to 3 minutes, or until mixture is thickened and translucent, stirring after every minute. Continue as directed.

◆ Look for Healthy Choice® products at your favorite supermarket.

Nutrition Facts	Amount/serving	%DV*	Amount/serving	%DV*	Menu Planning Guide
Serving Size ¹⁄₁₀ cake (134g)	Total Fat 5g	8%	Total Carbohydrate 40g	13%	One serving of this recipe provides: ½ Fruit
Servings per Recipe 10	Saturated Fat 3g	15%	Dietary Fiber 1g	6%	
Calories 219	Cholesterol 13mg	4%	Sugars 35g		
Calories from Fat 46	Sodium 111mg	5%	Protein 6g		

Vitamin A 10% • Vitamin C 2% • Calcium 8% • Iron 10%
*Percent Daily Values (DV) are based on a 2000 calorie diet.

Diet Exchanges:
2 starch • ½ fruit

APPLE RAISIN BRAN MUFFINS

1 cup bran flakes cereal with raisins

3/4 cup all-purpose flour

1/2 cup whole wheat flour

1/3 cup sugar

1 teaspoon pumpkin pie spice

1/2 teaspoon baking powder

1/2 teaspoon baking soda

1/8 teaspoon salt

1/2 cup nonfat or low-fat buttermilk

1/2 cup unsweetened applesauce

1/4 cup frozen cholesterol-free egg product ◆,
    defrosted, or 1 egg

2 tablespoons vegetable oil

1/2 cup chopped red cooking apple

1 dozen muffins

1 Heat oven to 400°F. Spray 12 muffin cups with nonstick vegetable cooking spray, or line cups with paper liners. Set aside.

2 Combine cereal, flours, sugar, pie spice, baking powder, baking soda and salt in large mixing bowl. Add buttermilk, applesauce, egg product and oil. Stir just until dry ingredients are moistened. Fold in apple.

3 Spoon batter evenly into prepared muffin cups. Bake for 20 to 23 minutes, or until lightly browned. Loosen muffins from rim of pan. Cool before removing from pan.

◆ Look for Healthy Choice® products at your favorite supermarket.

Nutrition Facts	Amount/serving	%DV*	Amount/serving	%DV*
Serving Size 1 muffin (58g)	Total Fat 3g	5%	Total Carbohydrate 22g	7%
Servings per Recipe 12	Saturated Fat <1g	0%	Dietary Fiber 2g	8%
Calories 122	Cholesterol <1mg	0%	Sugars 9g	
Calories from Fat 28	Sodium 122mg	5%	Protein 3g	
	Vitamin A 4% • Vitamin C 0% • Calcium 4% • Iron 15%			
	*Percent Daily Values (DV) are based on a 2000 calorie diet.			

Menu Planning Guide
One serving of this recipe provides:
1 Bread, Cereal, Rice & Pasta

Diet Exchanges:
1 1/2 starch

RHUBARB-BLUEBERRY COBBLER

2 cups frozen unsweetened rhubarb

2 cups frozen unsweetened blueberries

½ cup sugar

2 tablespoons plus 1 teaspoon cornstarch

2 tablespoons orange juice

¼ teaspoon ground ginger

1 cup light buttermilk baking mix

⅓ cup skim milk

8 servings

1 Heat oven to 350°F. In 2-quart saucepan, combine rhubarb, blueberries, sugar, cornstarch, juice and ginger. Cook over medium heat for 8 to 17 minutes, or until mixture is thickened, stirring frequently. Remove from heat. Spoon mixture into shallow 1½-quart baking dish. Set aside.

2 Combine baking mix and milk in small mixing bowl. Stir just until moistened. Drop mixture by tablespoonfuls onto fruit mixture. Bake for 28 to 34 minutes, or until topping is golden brown. Serve warm with low-fat ice cream or frozen yogurt, if desired.

Microwave tip: In 8-cup measure, combine rhubarb, blueberries, sugar, cornstarch and ginger. Microwave at High for 12 to 16 minutes, or until mixture is thickened, stirring every 2 minutes. Stir in juice. Continue as directed.

Nutrition Facts

Serving Size
⅛ cobbler (116g)
Servings
per Recipe 8
Calories 142
Calories
from Fat 12

Amount/serving	%DV*	Amount/serving	%DV*
Total Fat 1g	2%	Total Carbohydrate 32g	11%
Saturated Fat <1g	0%	Dietary Fiber 2g	7%
Cholesterol <1mg	0%	Sugars 18g	
Sodium 172mg	7%	Protein 2g	

Vitamin A 4% • Vitamin C 8% • Calcium 10% • Iron 4%

*Percent Daily Values (DV) are based on a 2000 calorie diet.

Menu Planning Guide

One serving of this recipe provides:
1 Fruit
1 Bread, Cereal, Rice & Pasta

Diet Exchanges:

1 starch • 1 fruit

ONION-PARMESAN BREAD STICKS

1¼ cups water
1 tablespoon instant minced onions
1 pkg. (16 oz.) hot roll mix
1 tablespoon vegetable oil
  All-purpose flour
¼ cup frozen cholesterol-free egg product ◆,
  defrosted; or 1 egg, beaten
¼ cup grated Parmesan cheese

16 servings

1 Combine water and onions in 1-quart saucepan. Let stand for 5 minutes to soften onions. Heat mixture over medium heat until hot (120° to 130°F). Remove from heat.

2 Combine hot roll mix and oil in large mixing bowl. Stir in onion mixture until combined and dough pulls away from side of bowl. Knead dough on lightly floured surface for 5 minutes, or until smooth. (Add flour as necessary to reduce stickiness.) Cover dough with bowl. Let rest for 5 minutes. Lightly spray 2 or 3 baking sheets with nonstick vegetable cooking spray. Set aside.

3 Heat oven to 375°F. Roll dough into 16 x 14-inch rectangle. Cut rectangle in half lengthwise. Cut halves crosswise into 1-inch strips. Twist each strip 3 or 4 times.

4 Arrange strips on prepared baking sheets. Cover with lightly greased plastic wrap. Let rise in warm place until doubled in size (about 20 minutes). Discard plastic wrap. Brush bread sticks with egg product. Sprinkle evenly with Parmesan cheese. Bake, one sheet at a time, for 12 to 15 minutes, or until bread sticks are golden brown.

Microwave tip: In 2-cup measure, combine water and onions. Let stand for 5 minutes to soften onions. Microwave at High for 1¼ to 2 minutes, or until hot (120° to 130°F). Continue as directed.

◆ Look for Healthy Choice® products at your favorite supermarket.

Nutrition Facts	Amount/serving	%DV*	Amount/serving	%DV*
Serving Size 2 bread sticks (53g)	Total Fat 2g	2%	Total Carbohydrate 22g	7%
Servings per Recipe 16	Saturated Fat <1g	2%	Dietary Fiber <1g	3%
Calories 119	Cholesterol 1mg	0%	Sugars <1g	
Calories from Fat 14	Sodium 230mg	10%	Protein 4g	

Vitamin A 0% • Vitamin C 0% • Calcium 4% • Iron 4%
*Percent Daily Values (DV) are based on a 2000 calorie diet.

Menu Planning Guide
One serving of this recipe provides:
1½ Bread, Cereal, Rice & Pasta

Diet Exchanges:
1½ starch

CRUNCHY COFFEE FROZEN TORTE

¼ cup hot water
2 tablespoons instant coffee crystals

2 pints vanilla nonfat frozen yogurt
   or low-fat ice cream ◆
8 chocolate sandwich cookies, coarsely chopped

10 servings

1 Combine water and coffee crystals in 1-cup measure. Set aside. Place frozen yogurt in medium mixing bowl. Let soften until yogurt can be stirred smooth. Add coffee and chopped cookies. Mix well.

2 Spoon mixture evenly into 8-inch springform pan. Freeze 4 hours, or until firm. Cut torte into wedges. Garnish with nonfat whipped topping and maraschino cherries, if desired.

◆ Look for Healthy Choice® products at your favorite supermarket.

Nutrition Facts	Amount/serving	%DV*	Amount/serving	%DV*
Serving Size 1 wedge (94g)	Total Fat 3g	4%	Total Carbohydrate 22g	7%
Servings per Recipe 10	Saturated Fat <1g	3%	Dietary Fiber 0g	0%
Calories 127	Cholesterol <1mg	0%	Sugars 15g	
Calories from Fat 23	Sodium 100mg	4%	Protein 4g	

Vitamin A 0% • Vitamin C 0% • Calcium 15% • Iron 2%
*Percent Daily Values (DV) are based on a 2000 calorie diet.

Menu Planning Guide
One serving of this recipe provides:
½ Milk, Yogurt & Cheese

Diet Exchanges:
1½ starch

ONION & GORGONZOLA STUFFED FOCACCIA

1 small red onion, cut into ¼-inch slices
1 small Vidalia onion, cut into ¼-inch slices
1 tablespoon plus 1 teaspoon olive oil, divided
1 tablespoon snipped fresh rosemary leaves
2 cloves garlic, minced
1 pkg. (16 oz.) hot roll mix

1¼ cups hot water (120° to 130°F)
¼ cup plus 2 tablespoons crumbled
    Gorgonzola cheese, divided

10 servings

1 Spray 12-inch round pizza pan or large baking sheet with nonstick vegetable cooking spray. Set aside. In 10-inch nonstick skillet, combine onions and 1 teaspoon oil. Cook over medium heat for 6 to 8 minutes, or until onions are tender-crisp, stirring occasionally. Add rosemary and garlic. Cook for 1 minute, or until flavors are blended, stirring occasionally. Remove from heat. Set aside.

2 Combine hot roll mix, water and remaining 1 tablespoon oil in large mixing bowl. Turn dough out onto lightly floured surface. Shape into ball. Knead for 5 minutes, or until smooth. Divide dough in half. Press half of dough into 11-inch circle. Place circle on prepared pan. Spoon half of onion mixture onto dough circle, spreading to within 1 inch of edge. Sprinkle evenly with ¼ cup cheese. Press second half of dough into 11-inch circle. Fit second circle over filling, pressing edges of focaccia to seal.

3 Heat oven to 375°F. Cover focaccia with cloth. Let rise in warm place for 10 to 15 minutes, or until focaccia is doubled in size and impressions remain when dough is pressed with 2 fingers to about ½-inch depth. Make indentations randomly in dough with fingertips. Top with remaining onion mixture and 2 tablespoons cheese. Bake for 25 to 30 minutes, or until golden brown. Serve warm in wedges.

Nutrition Facts	Amount/serving	%DV*	Amount/serving	%DV*
Serving Size 1 wedge (105g)	Total Fat 4g	6%	Total Carbohydrate 37g	12%
Servings per Recipe 10	Saturated Fat 1g	7%	Dietary Fiber 2g	8%
Calories 210	Cholesterol 5mg	2%	Sugars 1g	
Calories from Fat 36	Sodium 412mg	17%	Protein 7g	

Vitamin A 2% • Vitamin C 2% • Calcium 6% • Iron 8%
*Percent Daily Values (DV) are based on a 2000 calorie diet.

Menu Planning Guide
One serving of this recipe provides:
2½ Bread, Cereal, Rice & Pasta

Diet Exchanges:
2½ starch

RASPBERRY PIE

Crust:
- ¾ cup crushed vanilla wafer cookies (about 20)
- 2 tablespoons margarine, melted

Topping:
- 1 envelope (1.4 oz.) whipped dessert topping mix
  Skim milk
- 3 oz. nonfat or low-fat cream cheese ◆, softened

Filling:
- ½ cup sugar
- 3 tablespoons cornstarch
- 2½ cups fresh raspberries, divided
- 1 cup water
- ¼ teaspoon almond extract

8 servings

1 Heat oven to 400°F. In 9-inch pie plate, combine crust ingredients. Press crumbs firmly and evenly against bottom and sides of plate. Bake for 8 to 10 minutes, or until golden brown. Set aside.

2 Prepare dessert topping mix in small mixing bowl, as directed on package, using skim milk. At medium speed of electric mixer, beat in cream cheese until smooth. Set aside.

3 Combine sugar and cornstarch in 1-quart saucepan. Blend in 1 cup raspberries and the water. Cook over medium heat for 4 to 7 minutes, or until mixture is thickened and translucent, stirring constantly. Cool slightly. Stir in almond extract. Cool completely.

4 Fold in remaining 1½ cups raspberries. Pour filling into prepared crust. Spread topping evenly over filling. Chill until pie is firm. Garnish with additional fresh raspberries, if desired.

Microwave tip: In 4-cup measure, combine sugar and cornstarch. Blend in 1 cup raspberries and the water. Microwave at High for 5 to 6 minutes, or until mixture is thickened and translucent, stirring after 2 minutes, then every minute. Continue as directed.

◆ Look for Healthy Choice® products at your favorite supermarket.

Nutrition Facts	Amount/serving	%DV*	Amount/serving	%DV*
Serving Size 1 slice (128g)	Total Fat 6g	9%	Total Carbohydrate 32g	11%
Servings per Recipe 8	Saturated Fat <1g	5%	Dietary Fiber 2g	8%
Calories 190	Cholesterol 8mg	3%	Sugars 23g	
Calories from Fat 50	Sodium 156mg	7%	Protein 4g	

Vitamin A 6% • Vitamin C 15% • Calcium 10% • Iron 2%
*Percent Daily Values (DV) are based on a 2000 calorie diet.

Menu Planning Guide
One serving of this recipe provides:
2 Bread, Cereal, Rice & Pasta

Diet Exchanges:
2 starch • ½ fat

APRICOT BREAD

1 cup all-purpose flour
¾ cup whole wheat flour
½ cup packed brown sugar
1½ teaspoons baking soda
¼ teaspoon ground cardamom
1 cup nonfat or low-fat buttermilk
¼ cup frozen cholesterol-free egg product ◆,
    defrosted; or 1 egg, beaten
2 tablespoons vegetable oil
½ cup Grape Nuts® cereal
½ cup chopped dried apricots

16 servings

1 Heat oven to 350°F. Spray 8½ x 4½-inch loaf pan with nonstick vegetable cooking spray. Dust lightly with all-purpose flour. Set aside.

2 Combine flours, sugar, baking soda and cardamom in large mixing bowl. Add buttermilk, egg product and oil. Beat at low speed of electric mixer just until blended, scraping sides of bowl frequently. Fold in cereal and apricots.

3 Pour mixture into prepared pan. Bake for 45 to 50 minutes, or until wooden pick inserted in center comes out clean. Let stand for 10 minutes. Remove loaf from pan. Cool completely on wire rack before slicing.

◆ Look for Healthy Choice® products at your favorite supermarket.

Nutrition Facts	Amount/serving	%DV*	Amount/serving	%DV*
Serving Size 1 slice (46g)	Total Fat 2g	3%	Total Carbohydrate 21g	7%
Servings per Recipe 16	Saturated Fat <1g	1%	Dietary Fiber 2g	8%
Calories 110	Cholesterol 0mg	0%	Sugars 8g	
Calories from Fat 18	Sodium 125mg	5%	Protein 3g	

Vitamin A 10% • Vitamin C 0% • Calcium 2% • Iron 6%
*Percent Daily Values (DV) are based on a 2000 calorie diet.

Menu Planning Guide
One serving of this recipe provides:
1 Bread, Cereal, Rice & Pasta

Diet Exchanges:
1½ starch

HELPFUL HINTS
METRIC & U.S. MEASUREMENTS

One of the secrets of good cooking is to keep ingredients in their proper proportions. So whenever you use a recipe from this book, measure precisely if you want consistent success.

Measuring is easy with imperial utensils since quantities are listed according to the imperial system. Be aware, however, that U.S. liquid measures, used in these recipes, are not identical to their Canadian namesakes. For example, an American quart is about 8 (Canadian) ounces (1 cup) less than a Canadian quart.

Chances are, however, that imperial measurements on your kitchenware are according to U.S. standards. Since 1954, Canada's cooking industry standards for utensils (and recipes) have followed U.S. imperial measure (see below). As a result, the cooking quart is called the 4-cup quart, and a 5-cup quart is used to measure non-cooking liquids.

Of course metric utensils can also be used in preparing these recipes. Just maintain the proper proportions by measuring *all* ingredients according to the metric system.

GENERAL COOKING GUIDELINES

GRADING MEAT AND EGGS

The inspection marks "Canada Approved" and "Canada" mean the meat carcass was deemed fit for human consumption by a federal meat inspector. Any grade stamp (a colored ribbon) that might appear on the meat indicates the animal's age, color, texture, tenderness of cut and quantity of fat. Red ribbons indicate top quality, followed by blue, brown and black.

Grade A1 beef is the leanest and most tender, although all Grade A beef is well marbled. Grades B and C mean tougher flesh. Grade D is generally sold for processed meats.

Poultry is either Grade A, Grade B or "utility." Grade B and utility birds have imperfections that affect their appearance, or they are less meaty than Grade A poultry. They are best used in pies and stews.

Top egg grades are A1 and A. A1 eggs have a firm, high yolk centered in a clear, thick albumen. Use these for poaching or frying. The thinner albumen of Grade A eggs makes them more suitable for omelets or scrambling. Grade B eggs, occasionally available, are flatter and runnier still, with an off-center yolk, and are best used for baking.

TYPES OF MEAT CUTS

Canadian Meat Cuts	American Meat Cuts
Beef	
Beef sirloin tip roast	Beef round tip roast cap off
Beef blade roast boneless	Beef chuck eye roast boneless
Beef shoulder roast	Beef chuck arm pot roast
Beef wing steak	Beef top loin steak
Beef boneless shoulder roast	Beef chuck shoulder pot roast boneless
Beef sirloin steak	Beef pinbone sirloin steak
Beef blade steak	Beef chuck 7-bone steak
Beef inside round; beef top round	Beef top round steak
Pork	
Pork picnic shoulder roast	Pork shoulder arm roast
Pork loin roast, rib end	Pork loin blade roast
Pork cutlets, tenderloin end	Pork loin sirloin cutlets
Pork shoulder butt (or blade) roast	Pork shoulder blade roast
Smoked ham butt end	Smoked ham rump

COMMON CREAM VARIETIES

Type of cream	Milk fat (Canadian)	Milk fat (American)
Heavy or whipping cream (cartons)	About 35%	At least 36%
(cans)	18% to 26%	
Table cream	18%	
Half-and-half	About 11.5%	18% to 30%

REFRIGERATION TIME (Raw meat)

Ground meat	1-2 days	Roasts	3-4 days
Poultry	2-3 days	Steaks, chops	2-3 days

MEAT DONENESS
Internal Temperatures

Beef	140-170°F	(60-75°C)
Lamb	150-170°F	(65-75°C)
Pork	160-185°F	(70-85°C)
Poultry (thigh)	185°F	(85°C)
Veal	175°F	(80°C)

OVEN TEMPERATURE GUIDE

Celsius	80	100	110	120	140	150	160	180	190	200	220	230	240	260
Fahrenheit	170	200	225	250	275	300	325	350	375	400	425	450	475	500

METRIC & U.S. MEASUREMENTS

COOKING MEASURE EQUIVALENTS

Small Liquid and Dry Measure		Liquid Measure		Dry Measure	
¼ teaspoon	1 mL	1 fl. oz.	30 mL	¼ cup	50 mL
½ teaspoon	2 mL	2 fl. oz.	60 mL	½ cup	125 mL
1 teaspoon	5 mL	3 fl. oz.	100 mL	1 cup	250 mL
1 tablespoon	15 mL	4 fl. oz.	125 mL	2 cups	500 mL
1 coffee measure	25 mL	6 fl. oz.	200 mL	4 cups	1 Liter
		8 fl. oz.	250 mL		

DRY MEASURE

Ounces	Grams
1 oz.	30 g
½ lb. (8 oz.)	220 g
1 lb. (16 oz.)	450 g
2 lbs. (32 oz.)	900 g

LIQUID MEASURE (VOLUME)

Canadian Imperial Fluid Ounces (fl. oz.)	Metric Milliliters (mL)	U.S. Imperial Fluid Ounces (fl. oz.)
8 fl. oz.	235 mL	8 fl. oz.
	475 mL	1 pt.
1 pt. (20 fl. oz.)	570 mL	
	950 mL	1 qt.
1 Liter (35 fl. oz.)	1 Liter	34 fl. oz.
1 qt. (40 fl. oz.)	1137 mL	

EQUIVALENTS FOR COMMON INGREDIENTS

Food	Amount	Approximate Measure
Apples	1 pound (500 g)	3 medium-size
Bananas	1 pound (500 g)	3 medium-size
Bread crumbs, dry	1 slice bread	¼ cup
Bread crumbs, soft	1 slice bread	½ cup
Butter or margarine	¼ pound (125 g)	½ cup
Cheese, Cheddar	4 ounces (125 g)	1 cup shredded
Cheese, cottage	1 pound (500 g)	2 cups
Cheese, cream	3 ounces (90 g)	6 tablespoons
	8 ounces (250 g)	1 cup (16 tablespoons)
Flour, all-purpose	1 pound (500 g)	3½ cups unsifted
		4 cups sifted
Lemon	1 medium-size	3 tablespoons juice
		1 tablespoon grated rind
Orange	1 medium-size	⅓ cup juice
		2 tablespoons grated rind
Potatoes	1 pound (500 g)	3 medium-size
Sugar, brown	1 pound (500 g)	2¼ cups (firmly packed)
Sugar, confectioners'	1 pound (500 g)	4 cups unsifted
Sugar, granulated	1 pound (500 g)	2 cups

COOKWARE SIZES

Metric volume	Closest size in centimeters	Closest size in inches or volume
Cake pans		
2 L	20 cm square	8 inch square
2.5 L	22 cm square	9 inch square
3 L	30½ x 20 cm rectangular	12 x 8 inch rectangular
3.5 L	32 x 21 cm rectangular	12½ x 8½ inch rectangular
4 L	33 x 22 cm rectangular	13 x 9 inch rectangular
5 L	35½ x 25 cm rectangular	14 x 10 inch rectangular
Loaf pans		
1.5 L	20 x 12 cm	8 x 4 x 3 inch
2 L	22 x 12 cm	9 x 5 x 3 inch
3 L	25 x 12 cm	10 x 5 x 4 inch
Round layer cake pans		
1.2 L	20 x 3½ cm	8 x 1½ inch

Metric volume	Closest size in centimeters	Closest size in inches or volume
1.5 L	22 x 3½ cm	9 x 1½ inch
Pie plate		
1 L	22 x 3 cm	9 x 1¼ inch
Skillets or fry pans	25 x 25 x 5 cm	10 x 10 x 2 inch
	30 x 30 x 5 cm	12 x 12 x 2 inch
	33 x 33 x 5 cm	13 x 13 x 2 inch
Casseroles		
500 mL		20 fl. oz.
750 mL		24 fl. oz.
1 L		1 qt.
1.5 L		1½ qt.
2 L		2 qt.
2.5 L		2½ qt.
3 L		3 qt.
4 L		4 qt.

Index

CY DECOSSE INCORPORATED
A COWLES MAGAZINE COMPANY
Chairman: Bruce Barnet
Chairman Emeritus: Cy DeCosse
President: James B. Maus
Executive V.P. Creative: William B. Jones
Executive V.P.: Nino Tarantino

Healthy Choice ® is a registered trade-
mark of ConAgra Inc. used under license
by Cy DeCosse Incorporated.

CREDITS:
Design & Production: Cy DeCosse
    Incorporated
Test Kitchen Supervisor: Ellen Boeke
Home Economists: Ellen Boeke, Terry
    McDougall, Elizabeth Shedd
Editor: Janice Cauley
Senior Art Director: Delores Swanson
Art Directors: Mark Jacobson, Geoffrey
    Kinsey, Kathlynn Lehrke, Linda
    Schloegel

Project Managers: Diane Dreon, Kristen
    Olson, John van Vliet
V.P. Development Planning & Production:
    Jim Bindas
Production Manager: Laurie Gilbert
Director of Photography: Mike Parker
Creative Photo Coordinator:
    Cathleen Shannon
Studio Manager: Marcia Chambers
Photographers: Stuart Block, Rebecca
    Hawthorne, Rex Irmen, John
    Lauenstein, Bill Lindner, Mark
    Macemon, Paul Najlis, Charles
    Nields, Robert Powers
Contributing Photographers: Paul Markert,
    Brad Parker
Food Stylists: Bobbette Destiche, Beth
    Emmons, Nancy Johnson, Abigail
    Wyckoff
Production Staff: Kevin Heddin, Mike
    Hehner, Robert Powers, Mike Schauer,
    Nik Wogstad
Hand Model: Kay Wethern

Printed on American paper by:
    R. R. Donnelley & Sons Co. (1094)

Copyright © 1994
Cy DeCosse Incorporated
5900 Green Oak Drive
Minnetonka, Minnesota 55343
1-800-328-3895
All rights reserved
Printed in U.S.A.

Library of Congress Cataloging-in-
Publication Data

Recipes for Life® from the Kitchens of
Healthy Choice®
p. cm.
Includes Index.
ISBN 0-86573-941-2
1. Cookery. 2. Nutrition.
I. Healthy Choice Foods.
TX714.R4225 1994
641.5--dc20   94-12932